THE BOY AND OTHER STORIES

ROSSA SHERIDAN

For my early proofers, and most ardent supporters; Julie, Kirsten, and most especially, Doireann.

1

HOME

One of the most exciting events in our home every year was the day the TV cable man would come to cut us off. We never paid for cable TV. We never paid the government-mandated license fee either. When the license fee man came, my dad would just say, "We don't have a TV." This was utterly insane. Everyone had a TV. It was the 1980s; how would you watch *The Late Late Show* on a Friday without one?

The host of *The Late Late Show* was Gay Byrne. He was a God to the aul wans around Ballybough, although he wasn't God to my mam. TV was an excellent pastime, especially in the winter months when there was fuck all else to do with the aul lad in the theatre, or pub, or most likely both. So the license fee man got told we didn't have a television.

"I can actually see one in your window. There is a TV right there."

"Don't know what you're talking about," said my dad. "We don't watch TV in this house. Don't own one, and never will, so you can stop calling around here to check." A stare-down.

There wasn't much the lad could do, and I'm not sure he was in the right part of town, with his middle-class, South Dublin accent and his clipboard, to be asking Ballyboughers for money they didn't have.

The TV cable man, on the other hand, had a lot he could do. I don't know that I ever heard this lad speak, most likely because he really didn't have any need for speaking. He didn't ask if you were paying your monthly cable bill because he knew you weren't. He didn't need permission to cut you off, nor a courtesy verbal that that's what was happening.

Without warning, he swooped in like Batman, threw up the tallest ladder you'd ever seen, and cut the coaxial cable that ran into my mam and dad's bedroom before it snaked its way through the house, eventually sneaking downstairs to the living room, the front room in the house. The room where it was easy to see a TV through the window. After he'd cut the cable, he'd pull as much of it out of the house as possible, ideally leaving absolutely no cable at all to hook things back up again. But that's where my dad gained the upper hand.

After the first visit from the cable man, my dad rerouted the cable through the little vent in the brick that made up part of the bedroom wall. He tied three huge knots on top of each other just inside the bedroom so the TV cable man had zero chance of pulling any of the cable wire out of the house. That big knot was designed to get snagged in the wall, so the TV cable man would barely get a few feet of wire for himself. Reconnecting would be as simple as untying the knot, freeing up some cable slack, retying the knot for the next time he came by, and passing the loose end of cable out to be reconnected at the corner of the building.

So the next time the TV cable man cut our cable off in the summer of 1986, my Dad simply laughed it off. He watched him through the net curtain at the living room window as he leaned the ladder against the side of the house and climbed to the second story. Dad ran upstairs to the bedroom and chuckled silently into cupped hands as the cable man tried again and again to rip the coaxial wire through the little vent. Each time, the knots did their job and prevented him gaining even an inch, just like dad had planned.

My dad stood smug on the street as the cable man screeched off to his next appointment. He was hands on hips, secure in victory, but he wasn't aware that the job wasn't even half complete.

"Let's get the ladder around here," my dad said. "Let's get the TV hooked back up."

Our ladder was stored in our tiny back yard, but it was impossible to get it through the house to the street. The only path was over the back wall into the neighbors, through their field, out onto the street a hundred yards away, and all the way around to our house. Me and my brother dreaded having to do anything with the ladder, including carrying it around to the front of the house. I got caught in the ladder carrying crossfire this day, so me and my Dad dragged it over fences and through gates, and around to the front of the house.

We walked it up and positioned it under the corner of the building where the cut coaxial cable barely poked out from the vent in the red brick. But this was where my dad's difficulties started. The ladder was eight feet short of the vent.

"Bollox," said my Dad. "Yeh fucking bollox yeh. Hold the ladder, son. Let me see if I can reach it up there."

He scurried up the ladder, but it was obvious that even stretching at the last rung, he wasn't going to make it.

"Ok son, we need another plan. We have to get this connected back up or your mam will kill me."

He'd been arguing with my mam for the last six months that there was no way we were paying for TV, that it was easy to connect, and he'd take care of it if it ever got disconnected. Now he was under the kosh. If my mam didn't have the telly to watch while he was out at rehearsals there'd be absolute killings, and he knew it.

"How are we going to get up there?" he was muttering to himself. He definitely wasn't asking my opinion, and I knew, in this mood, it was better to leave him alone and let him solve the problem himself.

"How. In. The. Fuck. Are. . . I've got it. I've fucking got it."

"You," pointing at me, having briefly forgotten my name, I'm sure, as the plan formulated in his head. "Go inside and get four towels. Not the good ones, get some old ones, and bring them straight back out here."

I wasn't sure how towels were going to factor into the master plan, but I knew it was going to be fun to watch. When I returned to the street I wasn't sure if he'd lost his mind or was staging an accident. He had driven the VW Beetle up onto the path perpendicular to the house so it was just touching the wall.

"Roll up those towels, son, and hand them to me." he said.

He placed them where the windscreen met the body of the car, down where the wiper stems came out. We placed his altogether still-too-short ladder on the towels, and I watched as he inched his way up toward the top of the assemblage.

This was terrifying to behold. It wasn't so much that the whole thing looked rickety, it was that the slow speed and nature of keeping his center of gravity exactly over the center of the ladder brought one to realize there was no room for error here.

There *had* to be TV, and there *would* be TV, and no one was fucking paying for it. It was like a foreshadowing of reality TV in the following decade and beyond:

"What would you do for a free cable TV connection? Are you willing to pay with your life? We've collected twelve fathers from the Dublin 3 area and given them no instruction and shoddy tools, and tonight we're going to see who can become a hero and bring Gay Byrne back for the best *Toy Show* episode of *The Late Late* ever!!!!!!"

My dad always did reconnect the cable wire, and we were in business for another year. We watched mountains of sport—not the least of which was horse racing. We watched *Dallas* and *Dynasty* for a glimpse into the world of the American uber-rich, complete with the worst plot twist hitherto seen in a prime-time soap opera. We watched Saturday morning cartoons, all still Hanna-Barbera from the 1950s, followed by the British kids' shows on Saturday morning, and more on Saturday night. TV really was the center of our worlds.

* * *

My brother and I had several recurring errands we had to take care of—usually on a weekly basis—and one of these was to march a payment in the form of a cheque to the electrical appliance shop in Fairview, opposite Edge's Hardware, one of the most famous shops in all of Dublin.

My mam and dad had purchased a Video Cassette Recorder on the hire-purchase plan, and had to make weekly payments. The payments didn't seem like much at the time, but years later, as teenagers, my brother—who was a maths whizz—calculated that they must have paid close to a thousand pounds over three years before it was finally paid off. They ultimately paid well over three times the value of that piece of gadgetry, but in truth, if they hadn't signed up for that daylight extortion, they never would have brought it home at all.

And what an addition it was to our tiny little house in Bally-bough. We were on the cusp of the videotape rental boom, and my parents had somehow seen this clear as day. As soon as the machine came home, we were availing ourselves of the multi-tape rental over-a-few-day deals, and, like everyone else, we weren't getting to them all and would instead return most of the movies we took home.

There were forgotten tapes—reminded to us by the friendly teenagers working in the tape shop—and the ensuing negotiations, because no one could be expected to pay late fees for something that was no one's fault.

In the end, the tapes we ended up owning: my brother's football matches taped off the telly, and a copy of *Talking Heads: Stop Making Sense*, a concert movie directed by Jonathan Demme. It was pure genius—the cinematography, the direction and the coordination with the songs. Not dance, but yes, dance. It started with a raw, undressed stage, and a broom leaning against the back wall. Piece by piece, the stage components moved into position—a drum riser, the congas riser. Jerry Harrison took up his spot downstage on the third song. Finally, a blank canvas fully unrolled across the stage and the funkified songs kept coming, one after the other.

> Home is where I want to be
> Pick me up and turn me round
> I feel numb, born with a weak heart
> I guess I must be having fun
> The less we say about it the better
> Make it up as we go along
> Feet on the ground, head in the sky
> It's okay, I know nothing's wrong, nothing

IT WAS ROCK, it was funk, it was theatre, it was movie-making. It was a fucking revelation. I watched it a thousand times, and it was the piece of music most responsible for launching me into an unrelenting, impassioned, somewhat insane, lifelong love of music. There literally are no words to sufficiently explain how important the VCR, a complete waste of money, was for this kid.

2

VINNY'S GUITAR

The result of being two troublemakers from Ballybough was our exposure to the Dublin arts community. Our dad involved us in everything he was able to—not always out of desire. Sometimes, especially during the summer months, my mam needed a break from us, so my dad would take us to rehearsals, and we'd sit quietly in the auditorium while the actors, and my dad, the director, knocked a play into shape.

What was great about rehearsals was that the actors, knowing we were Gerry's kids, would talk to us generally like adults. Where were we going to school? Did we like it? Favourite subjects? Did we like music, and what bands? (me). How about sport—who do you support? (my brother).

They were genuinely interested in us, and in our intellect. We weren't treated like we were destined to get caught robbing a shop and end up in jail. We were treated like we were important. Like our interests had value. Like we mattered.

It was at one of these rehearsals when I was ten, that the actors took a break for a cup of tea. One of them had been playing an acoustic guitar as part of the show. I'd had my eye on it as an item of interest, and as soon as they broke, I leapt onto the stage and picked it up. Without any knowledge of the instrument, I started strumming the open strings, wondering how I could make the thing sound like the actor who'd been playing it so well had.

"Here, son," my dad said. "C'mere, let me show you something." I handed him the guitar.

"Ok, d'ya know this?" He picked the opening six notes of The Beatles' *Ticket to Ride*, then strummed the chord to finish. It was like magic to me. It hardly looked like he was doing anything, and yet I heard everything.

"Jaysus, that's bleeding deadly," I said.

He sat me down beside him and put the guitar in my lap.

"Now you're going to learn it," he said. "Put these three fingers here like this. You'll never get this wrong, because they all go right in here, on the second fret." I got my fingers into position.

"Ok, now just strum that chord."

I did, but it sounded muffled.

"Now, just make sure these fingers aren't muting any of the strings above or below."

It was hard. My fingers were hurting already, and he could see that they were.

"Ok, relax your fingers for a minute. Give them a little break, and when they feel ok, try again. I'm just grabbing a cup of tea—I'll be back out here in a minute."

I practiced the whole time he was gone. By the time he returned, I was ready for more. The more I played, the easier it got, and I was jonesing for the next notes to the tune.

"Great!" said my dad. "You're really getting it. Ok, now you're going to play the next bit like this. Pick this note here, then from the high E string back up these three strings. Now take your finger off here, play this string and the next string up."

It was hard, but there was an obvious pattern to it. Like a magician's trick, but easy to learn and remember.

"That's it!" said Dad. "Keep practicing that, and you have it. That's your first song!"

I think I'm gonna be sad, I think it's today, yeah
The girl that's driving me mad is going away, yeah

I had to give it up then, as rehearsals were starting back up again. I was fucking dying to get my hands on that guitar again. I knew part of a song! I wanted to practice and get better, and definitely learn that next chord. I think it's a D chord? Yeah, it even looks like a D!

Guitar became a new artistic and emotional expression for me. Finding space in the guitar's schedule got harder and harder and I became desperate. One night, the actor who owned it stopped into our house to say hello to my mam and dad. This was how people used to socialize in the old days. If you were in the area, you dropped in for a cup of tea and a digestive.

"Howareya Vinny?" I pressed as he came in the dining room door. "How's your guitar doing?"

Any info on my sweetheart was welcome. Maybe I could figure out a way to connect with her for a jam soon.

"Ah, Jaysus, I had to hock it, Rossa. I need the rent money this month. Maybe I'll get it back next month and I'll bring it around for you to borrow then?"

"Wait. You what?" demanded my dad.

"You didn't!" my mam stammered.

Vinny was a bit taken aback. I mean, it was his guitar after all. "I... I did. I fucking had to. I'm smashed broke, Gerry."

"But we would have bought it for Rossa!" blurted my mam, not mincing words as usual.

My heart sank. At least when Vinny had had it at his house, he'd bring it around, or I might be at the theatre with my dad, and I could practice *Ticket to Ride*. I had all three chords of the verse down and I was making great progress. It was hard to really keep making leaps when I only got to practice now and then.

"How much did you get for it, Vinny?" asked my mam.

"Fifty quid, Laura."

"Do you think you could get it out of hock, Vinny? If I gave you the fifty quid plus the extra, would you at least go see?"

FUCK YESSSSSSS!!!! I absolutely loved my mam right at that second. Both my mam and dad knew how much my new interest meant to me, how much I enjoyed it, and how quickly I was progressing when I had the opportunity.

"Yeah, Laura. No problem. I'm going to be in town tomorrow. Give us the money and I'll see what I can do."

"Laura, I don't think we have the—"

"We do, Gerry." my mam said in a tone of voice that meant, *We're not arguing about this in front of Vinny. We can discuss it later— but right now, this second, this is 100% what's happening.*

"There you go. Thanks, Vinny." My mam took the cash from her purse and handed it to him.

My brother was silent. This was very unusual, because in my house, neither of us could be given a bag of Tayto crisps without the other one screaming bloody murder for his packet. We'd cry how it wasn't fair, and ask, *Why does he get one and I don't?* And on, and on.

My parents even had a rule at Christmas—we gave them the money our granddad palmed to each of us, and they'd split it in half. Fair was fair, and my granddad's favouritism toward my brother wasn't going to pass muster in our house. There were always grumblings, but it was understood that this was how our family did business.

So this was major. This was a major purchase. A huge gift. This was a main Christmas present, before the stocking stuffers and such. This was massive. And for some reason, my brother was silent. It was as if he had had a similar realization: if this worked out, if Vinny managed to get that guitar out of hoc, this would be a gift beyond jeopardizing.

There was no room to scream for his share of the spoils here, and risk my mam saying, *Fuck it, no one's getting anything. Forget about it, Vinny—I thought I could do something nice for one of them, but apparently I was wrong.* The generosity of the gesture was beyond belief, and even a snotty 8-year-old understood that.

Needless to say, I came home from school a few days later and the guitar was in my living room.

"Go up and do your homework first, then you can play it."

"But MAMMMMMMMMMM!!!!!!!!!"

It was useless. I knew its addition to my house—at least on day one—would be leveraged to make me do my homework. I slammed the assignment out as quickly as I could and was straight into *Ticket to Ride* for the rest of the night in my bedroom; I was made to bring it upstairs immediately.

* * *

It was always a race in my house to answer the door. One never knew who it might be—an uncle, an actor, the odd now-famous but not-then-anywhere-near-famous artist, or someone from the flats selling stolen chocolate or jeans. So when the door knocker sounded one day, a few weeks after the great guitar gift, I threw myself down the stairs to answer it ahead of my brother. He barely lost that race to me, and we opened the door together to find a tall man in a suit and hat standing there. He was holding a folder containing some papers. He had what we'd now call a Burt Reynolds 80s mustache—but of course for the mid-1980s it was simply an epic mustache.

"Is your mam or dad home?"

We knew who this guy was. Although we'd never seen this particular man before, we'd had enough experience with debt collectors to know exactly who he was.

"Mam!!!! There's someone at the door!!!!!" My mam came out into the hallway from the dining room.

"Oh. Right," she said. "Kids, go inside."

My brother went inside, hardly concerned with this particular visit, while I ran up the stairs and hid around the first landing so I could spy on the conversation.

"Hello, Mrs. Fitzpatrick. I'm here to collect the fine for the TV licence. That'll be fifty-eight pounds today. Will you be paying cash?"

Of course it would be cash. There weren't any cheques in this run-down house.

"Mr, eh..." She stumbled for his name.

"Flaherty," he said.

"Mr. Flaherty. I know when we talked a few weeks ago, I said I'd have the money, and to be perfectly honest with you, I did have it there for a minute, but a, em, family emergency came up and, well, I just don't have it any more. I promise you if you can give me a couple more weeks, I'll have it then. I promise you."

"Ms. Fitzpatrick, if I'm being perfectly honest now, I'm supposed to be calling the Gardai and taking your TV right now. But in deference to your husband, who's a pillar in the community, I'm going to spare myself the headache and you and your kids the embarrassment. Mrs. Fitzpatrick, this isn't going to slide next time. I'll be back in two weeks."

Our family avoided a small disaster that day, and I learned how far my mam would go, and the bad fuckers she'd face up to, in order to provide anything for her kids so they could make headway in the world.

I still own Vinny's guitar. It's now back at my parents' house in Dublin, after having traveled across the United States with me. While living in Texas, I played small cafes with my friend Paul, whom I met in a park one night on a random wander around an Austin neighbourhood. And parties at my house (and others) in San Francisco, often with my mates from Ann Arbor, Michigan, who were all seriously talented players.

It's incredible how much an instrument can mean to someone. Those first few months of playing around Austin are embedded in the fibres of that guitar. Names have long since been forgotten but the smells, joyful vibes, and the crazy summer Texan heat will not be. The new tunes I played for Melissa, long gone - but not her name.

That guitar doesn't play so well anymore, but I'd never, ever let it go.

3

THE TRACKS

"Come on, for fuck's sake. Your ma and da won't find out," said Sean Crowe.

"Yeah yous saps. Do yous always listen to your ma and da? Do yis?" asked his younger brother, Keith.

Was there a stronger argument amongst kids than, *Do you always listen to your parents, you big baby?* It was all the convincing we needed. We wanted to go anyway—we just really didn't want to get caught.

Sean and Keith didn't have to worry about getting in trouble because their parents were never home. The only time I'd seen Sean and Keith's dad was when I was much younger. They lived on the third and highest floor of the flats, right at the very end of the block. Their flat was about as close to my house on Ardilaun Road as it was possible to get.

I envied Sean and Keith for their absolute freedom. Even if their dad knew they were on the train tracks, he wouldn't have cared. It didn't make sense, but some of their free rein seemed to rub off on us at that moment, and it became impossible to resist the peer pressure.

"Come on, fuck it then. Let's go," I said.

The four of us—Sean, Keith, my little brother, and me—headed for the train tracks near Clonliffe Road. We didn't even know where these ones went, but we assumed they headed down the country, like everything else leaving Dublin.

Sean pulled some coins from his pocket.

"Do yous have any money?" he asked. "You need a coin for the track, so the train can flatten it," said Keith.

We must have looked very puzzled in our silence, as Sean took a two pence piece from his pocket to show us. It was flat, slightly elongated, and twice as big as its original size.

"If you put it on the track, the train runs over it and turns it into that," said Sean. "It's brilliant, isn't it?"

For a family with an absent dad, and a struggling mam, Sean and Keith always seemed to have money. Every time I ran into them they had a pocket full of change. Sean was always trying to buy one of our toys from us. He always wanted to gamble by playing pitch and toss, where each player tosses a coin against a wall, and the player who lands their coin closest to the wall takes them both. It's no wonder he always wanted to play, because I genuinely never saw him lose. He was a toss savant.

Whenever my brother and I were fortunate enough to come across some money—like say, a handout from my granny—we spent it immediately on sweets in the local shop. I never understood how the Crowes didn't just spend their small fortunes, but instead hung onto them for pitch and toss, or squashing under trains. It was as if they'd discovered the joys of delayed gratification. Instead of just blowing it on chocolate and Coca-Cola, they used it to extend their interest in the world around them.

* * *

Sean gave me twopence, and Keith gave the same to my little brother.

"Righ, here, listen. When the train runs over them, they don't stay on the track. You have to watch them, righ? They're gonna jump off where they are. They might go under the train or they might jump off outside the track. If you don't watch them you'll fuckin' lose them. Yous owe that twopence back to us in anyway, righ?"

Sean had set the rules of the game, and the expectations for repayment of the stake, no matter the outcome.

"Does it matter where you put them, Sean?" I asked.

Sean and Keith both paused, bent over placing their coins, and looked at me sideways.

"How the fuck would it matter?" asked Keith. "Just put them on the track anywhere, but away from the other ones, so we don't get them mixed up." Or end up in a fight over whose was lost and whose was found, I thought.

We placed the coins and the wait for the train—whose direction of travel, destination, nor schedule was known—began in earnest.

Keith threw a rock at the plastic bottle we'd found on the side of the rail line. We'd set it up balanced on a sleeper, right in the middle of the tracks. He didn't so much throw the rock as sidearm it, as if he were trying to take out an enemy combatant. Missed.

Little brother's turn. Wide miss. We knew from his first several attempts that he wouldn't get close.

Now me. Close, but miss.

"Oooohhhhhhh," said Sean. "That was close, Fitzer. Do you want to bet on this one? I bet you 10p I knock it over."

"No thanks," I said. He'd already gotten really close with his first four or five attempts. It was actually amazing that he hadn't taken it out with the last throw.

Keith threw as hard as he could every time, while Sean's attempts were measured. He had calculated that power wasn't really part of the equation. His first shots seemed like markers—he was gauging distance. Hitting the bottle dead on would be ideal, but the margin for error on a direct hit was smaller than if he bounced the rock in front of the bottle and it sprung up to hit it.

Also, the tracks were covered in stones already. He was using this to his advantage, trying to career another rock up from in front of the target as well.

Each throw was identical to the last, like an Olympic archer who had spent years perfecting their technique to make it consistent—except that Sean was only on throw number six. There was no way I was betting against him.

Sure enough—BOOM—the bottle crashed over and some of the pebbles we'd used to keep it from blowing over in the wind came spilling out the top.

"Yeh fucking daisies!!!! Fucking BANG, you're dead!!! You owe me 10p, Fitzer!!!"

"My fucking hole," I said. "I never bet you, me bollox."

"Ah go on, it was still a deadly shot though, wasn't it?" asked Sean.

"Fucking deadly," said his brother.

"Deadly," my little brother and I said in unison.

"Will we go again? Everyone throw in 5p," said Sean. "20p to the winner!"

It felt like it was the winner's prerogative to request and be granted a betting wager, so we agreed, and set the bottle up to go again.

* * *

Just another day in Ballybough, then. Trying not to get obliterated by a train for the sake of flattening a two-penny piece. But there's so much more to doing nothing than doing nothing. Anything we could find to do was worthwhile. We had no money; we couldn't buy sweets or crisps or Coca Cola. We barely had a playground, and what was there had been vandalised beyond use. One of the older lads had set fire to the merry-go-round one night and melted it into oblivion. Incredibly, it still functioned, but it was lethal, and little kids often got their legs stuck underneath it. The only part of the playground that still worked as it was supposed to was the football pitch—iron tubing goals and concrete underfoot. It wasn't going anywhere.

I suppose we had each other, though, and no matter how utterly insane some of the kids from the flats were, you could always count on them for a laugh and an adventure. Today we were trespassing and attempting to employ a 60-ton locomotive to make the kind of coin souvenirs you could purchase at any funfair for 50p. It was equal parts ingenuity and stupidity, and we found that hilarious.

Several rounds of the bottle game later, we were getting into the swing of it. My little brother had been granted special privileges and got to stand twice as close to the target. He'd chalked up one win (albeit due to us letting him stand there and fling rocks until he finally connected). Keith had had a kill, and I'd had two. Sean was still the Olympic champion bottle-knocker-downer, with five kills to his name and at least 50p in earnings. But he was the only one counting the winnings at this point because we were all done with his brazen hustle. He couldn't hide it.

With no sight or sound of a train for the past hour, we'd all but forgotten the coins on the track. This is how our days typically went, though—a plan, an attempt to execute that plan, a change of plan because it wasn't going anywhere, and the creation of a whole new adventure to embark on. Over and over again. All we needed was a pallet, or an abandoned condiments factory, or a canal and fishing pole, or a river and a highly dodgy rope swing, or getting chased by a gang from another postal code or even possibly the most basic: a football and two jackets for goalposts. The cycle of adventure functioned sans anything to fuel it except our imaginations, some minor trespassing, our creativity, and whatever bits and bobs we came across along the way.

* * *

Keith stood the bottle up on the sleeper again. He'd knocked it over so he had to stand it up. Those were the rules, as they'd been written and reinforced by the game itself over the past hour or so. The mashed bottle had been severely abused, and it didn't really want to stand up anymore. It was attempting to surrender and accept its fate, but we didn't want to allow it just yet.

Keith gently nudged it into standing and removed his hand— palm facing the target—as if to coax it to remain in place just one more time. He stood slowly and turned towards us, but suddenly— arm still extended and palm still facing in the general direction of the sleeper—he froze. He was staring past us, down the track. In an instant, I feared the worst. A train was coming. Not really coming, but already here. It was twenty fucking feet from us, and it was too late. We were mincemeat. Maybe Keith could dive off the tracks and save himself, but it was too late for the rest of us. We were standing right between the rails. No one had really been looking out for trains, although we all agreed we needed to once the bottle game commenced. But we hadn't been, and now we were goners.

Instinctively, we turned toward the train. I expected it to be my final moment, but was relieved to find that I wasn't about to die horrifically— at least not at this instant. It wasn't a train. It was the Gardaí, and as soon as he saw us spot him, he broke into a trot.

"The fucking gards!" screamed Keith.

We ran, and we ran hard—directly away from him down the tracks toward the country. We hoped we wouldn't have to run that far to get away from him because most Gardaí stationed in Dublin were from the country, so it felt like the further down those tracks we ran, the further into his territory we were.

"Stop! Ye little fuckers!!"

Not a fucking chance, pal, I thought. I'm sure we all agreed. Getting caught on the tracks by the police meant getting the shit slapped out of you. It was a fate way worse than any legal ramifications or parental punishment could encompass. I once saw a Garda slap a friend of mine so hard across the face after a chase across a field in the local seminary (a top five adventure location), that he almost knocked him out. And our parents would thank them for it too—and then beat the shit out of us even more.

"Stop or you'll get the baton!!!!"

Yeah, we know. That's why we're legging it away from you.

This wasn't the first time we had been chased by the police, and we knew we had basically two options:

1 Outrun them ("him" right now, but sure to be more very soon), or

2 Get off these tracks, run back to the flats, and hide.

Luckily for us, we already knew all the ways off the railway.

"Let's get down at the hole in the fence at James's Avenue, near Croker," said Sean. We all knew exactly where this was. The added bonus here was it was a 12-foot drop from the fence to the street below. We knew that was no problem for us to jump down, and we also knew it was likely a huge problem for this garda. We were kids. We didn't give a fuck.

We'd squeeze through the chain-link fence, belly over, and then hang off the wall, and finally just let go and hit the street below. Our feet would sting like mad from the drop. We knew because we'd done it so many times before—just not under this type of pressure.

"You have to do this drop now, right?" I said sternly to my brother as we scurried down the embankment to the fence. He looked absolutely terrified. He'd never been able to do it before, despite all our encouragement. When we had a big group of lads, I'd always been the last before him, and had to wait for him to drop in case he couldn't do it. That way, there was someone to scramble back up onto the tracks with him and walk all the way around to the spot closer to our house that was easier to jump off.

"I'm serious," I said. "We're gonna get caught by the Gards if you don't do it."

He didn't even look at me this time. I could tell he was steeling his resolve for the task at hand.

"You first, Fitzer," said Sean.

"I'm gonna wait for my brother to jump," I said.

"No, you go first. Get down there to break his fall." Brilliant. Sean always seemed to think calmly in a crisis. I went.

Next was my little brother's turn. He was so scared he didn't even hesitate. I caught his fall a little bit, and he was fine. Next Keith, and finally Sean—and we were back on the street again.

The Garda didn't even bother climbing down the embankment to the hole in the chain-link fence. He knew he'd lost us. He just stood at the edge of the tracks, bent over slightly, hands on knees, catching his breath.

"You fucking wanker, you'll never catch us!!" Sean taunted him.

"Yeah, you're a fucking wanker," added Keith.

"We know all the secrets of the tracks!!! You don't know fucking anything, you prick!!!"

We ran from the tracks in the direction of the flats, as we didn't want to take any chances that reinforcements were on their way. But we knew that was unlikely—that the Garda on the tracks had zero chance of catching up with us—and we were safe.

"Oh fuck!" exclaimed Sean, as we trotted along Clonliffe Avenue. "The coins on the tracks!! Should we go back for them?"

He smirked, although he had us for a second.

We didn't want to take the chance that the Gardaí would swing by the playground in the flats to try to find us, so we camped out on a tiny strip of green grass nestled between the massive concrete wall of the final block of flats and, ironically, the massive concrete wall of the other set of railway tracks.

"That was bleedin' deadly," said Sean, and, motioning to my little brother, "You flung yourself off the tracks, you must have been shitting yourself! Are there any skid marks on your trousers? Turn around and give us a look, go on!"

"Fuck off, you, you prick. I'm bleedin' deadly at jumping off walls," he responded.

We debriefed, we laughed, and found fault with each other's

evasion tactics for an hour. There were belly laughs, and wrestling, and the worst impressions of each other, in turn, that had us laughing hysterically—so hard that some of the mams from the block of flats we were nestled up against popped their heads over their balconies to see just what the fuck was causing so much joy in this otherwise soulless environment.

4

LIVERPOOL

"I'm going," said Dad. He opened the dining room door to the hall and waited for Mam to look up from the crossword.

"Decoration used in a room for patients. A blank blank R blank?"

"Award," said my Dad.

"Brilliant," she mumbled as she filled it in.

"I'm going," he said again. "Are you going to say goodbye?"

"Yeah, goodbye. Have a good rehearsal, love."

"We will if the electricity stays on," he said.

He headed out into the freezing cold February night air, started up the Morris Traveler, and drove to the theater. This meant herding actors (some of whom had drinking problems and some of whom just had personality problems) into properly shaping his latest creation into the vision he'd had for years. It was to open in two weeks, and the actors were weeks behind on learning their lines. He was worried out of his mind.

It was easy to tell when my Dad was consumed with work. He vacillated between not hearing what you were saying or responding to you, and not acknowledging your existence. We were currently

past even that end of the scale and were somewhere near "I hope he doesn't drive into the canal," or "Has anyone checked if he's showered this week?"

My mother kept our world together. For a liberated 1960s feminist, she sure did a lot of laundry, shopping, and cooking. She also earned the only consistent income in our house, running a playgroup for the neighborhood kids. She charged next to nothing because it was all those parents could afford, but it meant that we had to go without as well.

It was the winter of 1982. I was ten and my little brother was eight. Ireland was in the depths of both a recession and a heroin epidemic that was destroying communities like ours. It was commonplace to step over junkies on the street who had nodded off on smack, as it was called. There was no money. There were no jobs. There was absolutely no hope for many young, working-class men, and the trappings of a smack habit—complete with purse-snatching and worse to maintain it—seemed inescapable. With no real social structure or older role models, the behavior of the younger teens in our community had gotten out of hand too. We were not immune to the destruction.

In mere seconds, I could hear the distant insanity rise from a whisper to a hurricane. The gang of 14- and 15-year-olds rounded the corner onto our little street, shouting and cursing.

"Mam, they're back," I said.

"Go into the dining room. NOW."

My Mam ushered us away from the window and into the other room. She followed, and almost immediately—*BANG*. Then *BANG*. *BANG*. Remarkably, the glass in the window had withstood the force of the rocks. Not content with that, one of them kicked the hall door twice, and ran off with his mates shouting:

"YOUS FUCKING WANKERS. WOODY ALLEN!!! POSH CUNTS!!!!"

Dubliners were known for the insanely brilliant nicknames

they invented. In this case, my dad had a receding hairline and wore glasses. He didn't look even the first bit like Woody Allen, but he was a writer—and that was good enough for the kids in our area.

When a heroin addict stole our car and crashed it 50 yards down the road, the police took my Mam aside and said: "Listen, we'll arrest him if you want. He's clearly guilty and he'll go to jail. But *you* have to live here. Think about it and let us know what you want us to do."

And of course, they were correct. Having that junkie arrested would have meant catapulting our family into an intolerable situation that could have meant unimaginable violence. We were already having our windows smashed and our front door kicked in for the crime of not being working-class enough. The bottom line in Ballybough: *Going to the police was not an option. No one snitched. Ever.*

* * *

My Mam was still in tears by the time my dad got home from rehearsals.

"Gerry, I'm in bits. A week of this—I can't take it. It's a miracle they haven't smashed the window or taken the door off its hinges."

"Yeah, I know," said Dad, first inspecting the door, then the window. "Fuck. What the fuck are we going to do?"

"Ok, boys. Bedtime!"

"But Mam!!!"

We knew there was going to be a hardcore adult discussion and we wanted to be privy to it. We wanted to know what the solution was going to be to this impossible-to-solve problem.

"BED! Are your teeth brushed?" (pointing to me).

"Yeah."

"Yours?" (pointing to my brother).

"Yeah."

"Ok, go. It's been a long day already. Good night."

Off we went, and although I tried to make out words from downstairs, I just couldn't. The best I could catch was that there were somewhat raised voices. But they weren't having a row. They were earnestly trying to work through the problem. By the time I fell asleep, they'd been talking for over an hour.

The following night was Saturday. The TV was great on Saturday nights—all the brilliant programs from the BBC. *Jim'll Fix It. Blue Peter.* My brother and I always got to watch them, and we almost always had my Mam's delicious homemade hamburgers and chips. It was a tradition, and we loved it. My mam was brilliant with child psychology. She knew that routine was the counterbalance to the environment we were growing up in, and we needed it now more than ever.

My uncle Francis, Mam's brother, called in. He stopped by a lot as he lived right around the corner. He and my parents sat in the dining room having a chat while we watched telly. Then there was another knock at the door and my uncle Paul walked in. Paul didn't really show his face in our house too often, and having him and Francis there together was definitely unusual.

As the night wore on, the adults got quieter. Soon, my mam said, "I hear them. They're coming."

Francis, Paul, and my Dad ducked out into the hallway. As soon as the first blow struck the door, they opened it and the boys scattered. The men sprinted out after the gurriers and Francis caught a couple of them on the next street over; my Dad caught one on a street over in the other direction. Soon they returned to the house.

"That's the last you'll hear from them," said Paul.

"Yeah, well, maybe," said Dad.

"Ah come on, I slapped the bollox out of that one I caught. He won't try that again," said Paul.

"I headbutted that little prick. His fucking nose exploded," said Francis. "They'd be fucking stupid to fuck with yous again."

"There'll be repercussions," said Dad.

It took 30 minutes.

There was a respectful *knock knock knock* at the door.

"Stay inside, Laura."

My Dad went and opened the door. Standing outside was Mark Scally—one of the scariest drug dealers to ever walk the earth—the smell of several pints of beer on his breath. Beside him, was his 14-year-old brother Joey. Joey's nose was destroyed. There was blood all over his face, his jacket, his hair. It looked like he'd run into a wall at full tilt.

"Alright?" said Mark.

"Howareya?" said Dad.

"Did you do this to my brother?"

Mark was speaking to my Dad, but he was staring at his brother —not quite believing what he was seeing.

"I did," said Dad.

He hadn't, in fact. It had been Francis' headbutt that had done the damage—but it was understood that my Dad was responsible for everything that had happened that night.

"Do you mind telling me what for?"

Mark's diction now increased in politeness, and hinted at the sheer terror that might be coming next.

"Well, yeah," said Dad. "I will tell you. Your brother and several of his mates—for the last week now—have been coming down the road and terrorizing my family. They've been throwing stones at the window and kicking in the door. We're only trying to live here in peace. I've been out at the theater at night, and Laura is fucking terrified in there."

Mark, who hadn't taken his eyes off his younger brother, said: "Is that true?"

"Yeah, Mark—" Joey hardly had the words out of his mouth before Mark leveled him with an open-handed slap to the face that was as loud as any of the window assaults from the last week.

As Joey got back to his feet, Mark said in a low tone, "Say fucking sorry."

Joey, now crying, said, "I'm sorry." Tears streamed down his face.

"Hang on a minute, you little fucking prick. Getting me out of the pub for this bollox." For the first time since the assault, Mark turned his gaze back to my Dad.

"Gerry, isn't it? You're the writer, yeah?"

"That's right," said my Dad.

"Say fucking sorry to Gerry, you little prick."

"Sorry, Gerry," said Joey.

"Go straight back to the house and wait for me there. I'm not done with you." Joey turned and headed down Sackville Avenue, towards the middle block of flats where he lived with his parents, his older brother Mark, and several other siblings.

"Gerry, you helped my Uncle Larry, didn't you?"

"Larry? Yea, I ran the community acting workshop he was in. It let him keep his dole, and I recommended him to the Abbey Theatre for that ushering job he's had since," said Dad. "So yeah, I know him."

"Yeah, I thought so. Listen, I'm really sorry for all the shite you've had to put up with this last week. I'm going to send someone around to check your window and door, and if there's any damage, it'll be fixed, ok? Just one other thing, Gerry—I'd like to discuss something with you. Would it be ok if I came back around tomorrow night?"

"Yeah, whenever you like, Mark. Tomorrow is fine. I'll see you then," said Dad.

* * *

It seemed like the best possible—and worst possible—outcome to a horrible situation.

Dad came back inside and propped my little brother on his knee.

"Was that scary earlier?" he asked.

The tears stained my brother's ruby cheeks, and he looked like he was about to burst into floods again.

"We won't ever have to worry about those kids breaking our windows again, d'ya hear me? I promise you, that's over now. Forever."

It really felt like, given the hiding Joey had gotten—first from my uncle, and later from his own brother—that we were safe from being terrorized again.

Mark Scally wanted to meet with my Dad. This couldn't be good. There was no way this could shake out in a positive light. Mark Scally barely knew who we were. What did he want with us? What did he want to talk about?

It clearly couldn't be anything to do with Joey—he'd already slapped Joey for the hassle he'd caused our family. But this was the conversation between my parents all day Sunday—almost rising to a row at times.

"I don't fucking know what he wants, Laura. If I knew, I wouldn't be so fucking freaked."

They tried to kill time by taking us to the playground, but it was full-on silence and pale faces all day and into the evening. After dinner they came up with the lamest excuse ever: "It's Sunday, and you've school in the morning, and I don't care what time it is—you have to go to bed. *Now.*"

But we knew that Mark Scally was coming around for something—and no one knew what. Everyone was on pins and needles.

I had only one thing in mind, and it depended on my brother being asleep by the time Mark showed up. My plan was to sneak out of the room and sit at the top of the stairs, where I might be able to hear the conversation in the dining room below. I couldn't pull this off if my little brother was awake—he wouldn't understand the gravity of the situation and would make a bunch of noise and give away our position. Luckily, he was out by the time Mark arrived. I crawled out of bed, sat down at the top of the stairs, and settled in for the show.

The voices downstairs were hushed, and it was next to impossible to make out what was being said. For a bad man, Mark really spoke quietly.

The whole thing couldn't have lasted more than 15 minutes, and it seemed like Mark had done most of the talking. The only giveaway was when the meeting was over and Mark went to leave. My Dad walked him to the front door to let him out.

"Once, Mark. I can do it once. But this is not my specialty. I'm a writer, for fuck's sake."

"Next Saturday then, yeah?" said Mark as he closed the door behind him.

* * *

The sun was just rising as the ship pulled away from the dock on Dublin's North Wall and pointed itself northeast toward Liverpool. Our excitement was at an all-time high. My brother and I walked around the passenger seating area, checking out every single detail of the boat.

It wasn't long before we seemed to catch our cruising speed and left Dublin's eastern shore behind. The sea air felt amazing out on the passenger deck. The spray was saturated with salt. We tasted it on our lips—the taste of something entirely new. We jumped in the air trying to time our leaps to catch the spray in our mouths, but the boat had started to bounce around, and it was getting harder to time it properly. Our landings were almost impossible. We inevitably fell and laughed and scrambled up in time for the next try.

Dad said, "Get in here now! It's too rough for that, lads."

It really was getting rough—more so than the advertisements in the newspaper had promised in the run-up to the trip:

Travel from Dublin to Liverpool by Hovercraft on the Jetfoil! Balanced on a cushion of air and moving twice as fast as the car ferry. No seasickness. No cancellations

Within 15 minutes of coming inside, my brother and I had thrown up several times.

We were headed to England to see a First Division football match. This was the pinnacle of world soccer—or at least, the pinnacle of English soccer.

My brother had been a Liverpool fan since what seemed like his first words. So it was definitely a surprise when our Dad told us about the last-minute trip, and revealed that we were going to see Everton F.C.—Liverpool's crosstown rivals—play Wolverhampton Wanderers. These clubs weren't just rivals. They *hated* each other. Many fans wouldn't even speak the name of the other club.

Now, my brother was only eight—but if you were going to the effort of taking the puke boat to England, surely you'd plan the trip so he could see *his* club. Any two random clubs for a great day trip to England— yes, sure. But *Everton*? The hated Everton?

The football match was incredible. It finished 1–0 to Wolves, the only goal scored by Emlyn Hughes, a former Liverpool captain now playing for Wolves, a massive star at the time. Most significant was the crowd—the sheer *size* of the crowd—and the feeling that anything could kick off at any moment. Everything felt fragile.

We got back to the Jetfoil later that day in time for the departure. People were milling about, buying snacks from the handful of vendors. My Dad fumbled around in his pocket and slipped me some coins.

"Go on over to your man there and buy a couple of ice creams for you and your brother," he said. We sprinted over to an ice cream stand and picked out our favorites.

"That'll be twenty pence," said a man who I immediately thought might have been the father of all four Beatles.

I tried to pay, but he wouldn't take the money.

"No son, you need English money. That's Irish money you've got there."

Fuck. What the fuck was my Dad giving me the wrong money for?

We handed John-Paul-George-O back the ice cream and turned to head back.

"Dad, you gave us the wrong money!!!" we cried in unison.

He wasn't paying attention. Now, normally, he had to be in work mode to fall into such a stupor so this was unusual.

"Dad!!! Dad!!! You gave us…"

"Hang on kids, I'm just looking for someone."

Who could he be looking for?

The boat had boarded and was honking its horn, indicating to any stragglers that the gangplank would be pulled up shortly. But we were still standing on the dock with my dad in a mind of his own.

"Who, Dad? Who are you looking for?"

My brother was only eight, and I was only ten, so we couldn't help our Dad look for his friend, even if we wanted to. We were too small to see over any of the heads milling about the dock. And anyway—we didn't *know* who we were looking for. It seemed our Dad didn't even know.

Then—*bang*—his eyes locked on someone, and his hands, which we had been holding, squeezed ours.

"Gerry!!!! Jaysus, howareya Gerry??!?! And your little fellas!!! How are yis? How was Everton? They're bleeding deadly, aren't they? Did they win today?"

"Lads, this is Larry. Say 'hello Larry'. I don't think you've met him before. He lives down on Rutland Street."

"Hiya Larry! Hiya Larry," we said.

Larry swung a big black duffel off his shoulder and dropped it with a thud onto the concrete.

"I'm glad I caught yis," he said. "I got something for the boys." Larry hunched down and unzipped the duffel and slid out a white bat with a black taped handle. "Here you go lads—I bought you a cricket bat! Now, share it and take turns, ok? No arguing over it."

"Is that everything, then?" my Dad asked.

"Yeah. That's all," said Larry.

My Dad turned toward the boat—but suddenly Larry had a grip on his arm. My Dad looked down at the hand, puzzled, then back at Larry.

"We're going to miss the boat, Larry. What are you doing?"

"Give it a second," said Larry. "Just wait a second, ok? You'll still make it, let's just make sure you board at the last second. You won't be searched if you're last to board."

Turning again to the boat, the customs officials blew a final volley of whistles and fired up the machine to hoist the huge gangplank.

"Jesus Christ! Yous are going to miss the boat!!!" Larry shouted. "Kids, run and have them hold the boat for your Dad!"

We sprinted straight to the gangplank, and Larry released his grip on my Dad's arm and said:

"Now. You're in the clear. Go."

The customs men halted for a few seconds, waved us up the ramp, and gave my Dad just a cursory pat-down before making their final checks.

* * *

The three of us settled into two seats and prayed we wouldn't get the waves like we'd had on the way over. My dad was wrecked. But he took us in turns onto his lap and bought us crisps and chocolates and Club Orange from the concessions. We had just had the best day of our lives.

Cricket is an English game. We would have preferred a football to a cricket bat. It was a source of contention—at least for the ferry ride home.

We got home after our momentous day abroad and crashed

hard. We couldn't find the bat the next day. We searched every-where, but we had other activities to keep us busy, like riding our BMX bikes.

My dad had only one week left to get the play opened after we returned from Liverpool. He was away with the fairies that entire week. I don't think he even knew anyone in the family's name—but it hardly mattered, because he was out of the house all day and all night.

Finally, the show opened to a smashing reception. My little brother and I were just old enough to attend. It was amazing—there was all the red lemonade we could drink, and we had a burping competition. We're still arguing over who won.

On opening night, my dad was surrounded by people: "Con-gratulations!" and "Well done, Gerry!" You could tell he was delighted—for the actors, for the theater, for everyone who'd been part of it. But he was shattered too. He looked like he needed a week of sleep.

The following afternoon, two men arrived at the door. My dad seemed like he had been expecting them. He asked us to go outside and play football for a while so they could chat in private.

After they'd left, we came back in and found a Bible and some pamphlets on the dining table. My dad told us he was going to stop drinking for a while because he wasn't sure he was being the best father to us at the moment.

Then he started crying. It was the only time I ever saw my dad cry. My brother and I ran to him and hugged him, and the tears flowed even harder.

The incident with Mark had shaken my dad to his very core. He always claimed he only ever had a few pints after rehearsals, or when meeting someone for work - which meant nearly all the time. He realized that he could no longer place his life, and the lives of his family, in the hands of the lunatic drug dealers in Ballybough. He needed to get us out of there, and he couldn't do it drunk. So he got honest with himself, placed his faith in the program, and surrendered to God.

We only lived on our little street in Ballybough for less than a year more. We left soon after, to a nicer, bigger house a couple of miles out of the inner city. Just after my dad got sober.

Within seven months, he had accomplished what had seemed impossible for over a decade. He had moved us away from the madness. And with his own rebirth, he offered one to us, too.

5

CHRISTMAS

We knew we'd heard it. Santa's sleigh on our roof. My mam said if we didn't go to sleep that he'd arrive, and he'd know that we were still up, and he'd fuck off to the next house and not leave us any presents, despite the bottle of Guinness and biscuits we'd left downstairs on the dining room table. But now, here he was. And he was going to know we were still awake and acting the maggot. Santa was magic, so you couldn't fool him. He knew everything, especially at this time of year. He knew if you were doing what your mam asked, or if you were being a little shit. You couldn't fool him, so what choice did we have now?

"That's Santy," I said to my brother in the bottom bunk. He was motionless. Silent.

"Pretend to be asleep," I whispered. Finally, the late hour and the adrenaline crash—from what I will still claim to this day was Santa's sleigh skidding across our roof—had caught up with us. The quiet night swallowed us and spat us out mere hours later, as the adrenaline built once more.

BMX bikes. Fucking deadly. But these were not the Raleigh Burners we'd asked for and were de rigueur amongst the BMX riders of 1985 working-class Dublin. These were no-names. They were yellow and gaudy, unlike the stylish Raleigh Burners all our mates had. Our friend Terrence, from across the road, even got the model up from a Burner because he was an only child, my mam said, and because his dad was always away and probably felt guilty. Our dad was always around, on the other hand, and probably didn't feel at all guilty about buying us these bright yellow no-name bikes. We were sure to get a massive slagging later on the road.

That would have to wait, though, because it was still six o'clock in the morning, and that particular reconnaissance trip had been a fact-finding mission only. An inventory-gathering exercise. We had stockings in our bedroom, hung from the end of our beds, filled with torches and mandarin oranges, a wristwatch, and some choco-lates too. But we had wanted to know what we'd scored for our big presents, under the tree in the living room. We had hoped to discover those red-and-black Raleigh Burners, and it was equal parts disappointment and acceptance we felt as we heard our mam stir in her bedroom above the living room.

We froze and looked at each other. Often, one of us would have a way out of trouble. Eye contact would decide the lead that was best to follow. But there was no getting out of this one. My mam was going to absolutely kill us for being up so early on Christmas morning, and more to the point, for waking her up. The best strategy now was to remain further out of her reach than my brother, but as she thundered down the stairs that became impos-sible too. The dining room door slammed open, and in an incredu-lous tone, at a volume and intensity that betrayed the seriousness of waking either of my parents up before 11 a.m. on any day that didn't require them to be up at all, she growled, "Get the fuck back up to bed. It's the middle of the fucking night."

As soon as my mam settled back to sleep we figured it was safe to whisper a conversation. I leaned out of the top bunk so I could see my brother in the bed below.

38 ROSSA SHERIDAN

"What'd ya think of the bike, then?" I asked.

"'S alrigh'," he said.

"I can't wait to do a load of wheelies on it later," I said.

"Yeah," he said. "Me too. Maybe we can have a wheelie competition?" he whispered.

"Definitely," I said. "And, don't forget, bunny hops off the path."

We were trying to talk ourselves out of the disappointment of not getting the Raleighs we wanted, while at the same time, anticipating that although they weren't the coolest, functionally we'd be getting the same enjoyment from them, specifically, the adventures and freedom that first bike affords a young rider.

For now, the only thing to do was consume all of the chocolate and mandarin oranges in our stockings, and use the torches to crack open the books we'd gotten. We'd read until we couldn't stand it any longer. We knew once it got somewhat light outside, our mam and dad would tolerate us making noise downstairs, and in fact, would come down to unwrap some of our other gifts with us, and make sure we were okay bucking up and down the street on the new yellow speed machines.

* * *

We lived in number 2 Ardilaun Road, and Michael Dunne lived in number 1, right next door. The house numbering didn't follow any fancy odd-this-side, even-the-other-side system. It was as if they had just thrown the houses up around the turn of the 20th century, started at 1 and ended at 7 or 8, a little further down past the flats, where the huge wall demarcating the train tracks cut off any further possibility of construction. It seemed to imply that this would be a good place to stop thinking of any further escape from Ballybough.

Michael, as I'd learn as I grew into adulthood, was a watchmaker—retired now and well into his 90s. He was barely alive, and I don't think I ever saw him venture out of the house. Confined to a single room, he'd been abandoned by his own family. We were the only people he had any contact with at all, aside from a trip to the shops for tea, milk, bread, and butter once per week.

We had seen people visit him occasionally. We'd assumed they were relatives, but upon talking to Michael, he said they were old work colleagues from Switzerland, and they'd come to visit to discuss a design problem they couldn't solve.

"Did you help them, Michael?" my Dad asked.

"I did of course, Gerry. They were very happy."

There were occasions when Michael had a turn and fell and came to my dad for help. We'd assist him back to the front room of his house. It would have been the living room, as it was in our house, where many years earlier he'd set up a bed and a small table with a kettle. The stench from the piss-soaked mattress was overwhelming. This was where Michael lived—and where he would eventually die.

The houses on our row were originally built with outhouses in the back gardens. Our house, plus the others, had kitchens constructed off the back of the house to connect to the outhouse, which was revamped into a bathroom. The only house on the block that had never undergone this remodel was Michael's, and so, from my bedroom window at the back of our house, I would often spot his bald, scarred head shuffling out his back door and through the weeds, toilet roll in hand, making his way down to the outhouse.

Michael lived his entire adult life in that house. On the 21st of November 1920, when 14 people were shot by British Forces while attending a GAA match in Croke Park—which our houses backed up onto—some of the injured were carried up over Michael's back wall and into his house, where they received treatment while waiting for ambulances. I estimated once that Michael had been born around 1890, so he would have been a young man of 30 at the time. He was quite literally from another time and place in history, and he sure seemed like it to me and my brother. What a shock when my Mam told us that Michael would be joining us for Christmas Day, and dinner.

Our Christmases were always the same—it was me and my brother, my mam and dad. We played with our new toys, watched TV, ate way too much sugar, and of course, had Christmas dinner around 5 or 6. It wasn't supposed to include some old man who'd been given my mam's armchair to sit in, and was constantly being asked if he wanted another Guinness or a bite to eat, and him going "EEEEHHHHHHH???" because at 96 he was almost completely deaf. My dad had to shout the question at him again.

"DO YOU WANT A PIECE OF FRUITCAKE TO GO WITH THAT STOUT, MICHAEL?"

I understood the idea—he had no one. He probably hadn't had a Christmas with another living soul in decades. But why did it have to be us?

Of course, it had to be us, because there was no one else on our little block of four houses that was capable of taking him in. The rest of the neighbors were in their 70s and had probably just managed to pull together a dinner themselves.

For me, the problem with Michael was his age, and the fact that he was potentially seconds from exiting this plane. It was terrifying for a 12-year-old to be that close to a human person who could check out at any time. Although he was very much alive, if he'd keeled over right then and there, it honestly wouldn't have been a shock to anyone.

He was probably very lucky to have found a profession in horology. Michael would have known famine survivors—people who still carried it in their bodies—and would have felt lucky to have been born just 40 years later, and to have found a profession that he absolutely excelled at. As a genius watchmaker, he travelled back and forth to Geneva when his countrymen and women—if they boarded any vessel out of the country—were unlikely to ever return.

They needed him. He had skills and knowledge. And when

they'd mined him for it, they sent him back to his tiny little house two miles from town, in an area yet to be developed with massive brutalist blocks of flats housing for Dublin's working class.

"There you are, Michael."

"HUUHHHHHH?" he grunted.

"Ah, Jaysus," said my Dad.

"YOUR STOUT AND YOUR FRUITCAKE, MICHAEL. I'LL LEAVE THEM HERE ON THE ARM," shouted my dad as he balanced them precariously on the arm of my mam's armchair. There was nowhere else for him to put them. The room was cluttered with toys, and Michael wouldn't have had the dexterity to reach down and pick either of them up off the floor. And to be honest, I'd say he would have forgotten they were there within a couple of minutes.

"Gerry!" Michael strove to grab my Dad's attention as he walked away.

"YES, MICHAEL!" said my Dad. More of a statement than a question, at that volume.

"I once sat on the lap of James Joyce. Did you know that? I was only a youngfella. Maybe his age." He gestured at my 10-year-old brother.

"YES. YOU TOLD ME THAT BEFORE. HE DIDN'T SAY ANYTHING TO YOU, MICHAEL? ANY WORDS ON HOW TO WRITE WELL?"

"Sure I don't remember, Gerry. I wish I could remember."

We'd heard it all before.

Poor Michael—abandoned by his family years ago, living in a single room and sleeping on a piss-soaked mattress, with only his pension to keep him afloat from week to week. That and the faint memories of a life lived.

* * *

Knocking on the living room window was standard in our

house. It must have started back when we were very young, when the door knocker would have woken us up. My parents had their relatives and friends coming around for drinks and parties well into their 30s, so people started knocking on the living room window so as not to wake us up—even when we were still actually up and about. No one used the knocker at night time, and during the day, it could only be someone unfamiliar with our family.

It was a complete shock, then, when at 3 a.m. on Christmas night, Michael Dunne was pounding at our window and shouting,

"Gerry, Gerry, Gerry!!!!"

My mam and dad rushed down the stairs, opened our front door, and ushered Michael through the hallway and into the dining room, where mam switched on the lights to reveal the frail man in a complete panic, blood running down his face from a gash on his temple.

"MICHAEL, DID YOU HAVE A FALL?!?" my dad asked frantically.

"MICHAEL, YOU MUST HAVE HAD A FALL?!" my mam said.

"Get him a glass of water, Laura," said my Dad.

"I'll get it," I said.

They both looked at me— wishing I hadn't witnessed the scene, and at the same time, accepting that no one had a choice in the matter.

I handed him the glass, which I'd only half-filled, knowing he'd find it hard to hold onto it at all. I wrapped my hands around his and helped him raise it to his lips. Something had changed in me with respect to my feelings towards Michael. Until now—and even, in fact, until earlier the previous day, Christmas Day—I'd felt scared of Michael. He represented everything I wanted to steer clear of: death, fragility. Something had shifted in me since. I understood his life was as cherished and precious to him as mine was to me. He'd really lived, and even if he couldn't remember most of what he'd done, he didn't deserve to lie abandoned by his closest kin, just waiting for him to die so they could inherit his house. It was shit, and I felt overwhelming empathy for him.

He raised the glass to his lips, hands shaking.

"You fell, Michael?" my dad said softly.

"How did you fall?" asked mam.

"I was robbed, Laura. Gerry. I was robbed. They told me they were the police and I needed to open the door, and when I did, they pushed me over . . ." Tears of fear and confusion were streaming down his face now.

"He's had a nightmare or something," said my dad. "Or he tripped going to the outhouse. I'll go in there and make sure everything is okay. Maybe I can see where the blood is and what he might have tripped on. Put on the kettle," he said to my brother, "and make him a cup of tea. Laura, can you get him onto the couch in the living room? "You," he said, pointing at me, "you come with me."

The eight steps that led from our front door to Michael Dunne's front door could never have let on what we were about to find. As my dad put it later: "If you'd given me a free 1,000-to-1 bet for a tenner, I never in a million years would have guessed. I mean, it's still just a complete stunner. It's the stuff that plays are made of!"

Reaching that doorway and making that left turn into Michael's hallway confirmed he'd told us the truth. Money was scattered down the stairs and into the hall, as if a safe had exploded. There were notes and coins of every denomination, sure. But it wasn't just pence and pounds—there were other kinds of notes with old Irish writing on them. The place looked like a museum had been robbed.

"He was robbed after all," said my dad. "Close that front door, son, and stay beside it. I'm going to take a quick look upstairs."

In no time, he was back downstairs.

"Okay, son," he said, "I've got to think quickly. What are we going to do here? There's fucking thousands upstairs, thousands down here too."

Michael Dunne had been hiding a secret—and that was that he had more money stashed in cardboard boxes underneath a bed in an upstairs bedroom than anyone in our community had to their name.

"What are these notes with the old writing on them, Dad?" I asked, hoping to interrupt his thought process.

"Old money, son. Old money. That was the money your Da used when he was your age. It hasn't been in circulation since 1971. Look, this is a shilling, the one with the bull on it. And this one, with the salmon—that's a florin. That symbol was used to represent the salmon in Irish mythology where the Salmon of Knowledge swam in the Well of Segais. Jaysus, there was no fuckin' sign that this money was in this house, was there?"

It was a simple calculus for my dad: pack up and spirit away some of the new money, or leave everything as was and call the police. It was obvious that, after a day with Michael in our house, we were the only family he had. So maybe it wasn't the worst thing to liberate a small amount of this unused stash. The upshot of leaving it was that Michael's absent relatives would be only too happy to come 'help' him secure it someplace. But that would be the last anyone would ever see of it.

"Son, there's a lot of money here, but none of it is ours. And no matter what Michael has chosen to do with it over the course of his lifetime, that's been his choice. We're going to leave the place exactly as is so the police can inventory it, and dust for fingerprints —or whatever it is they need to do. Let's go back inside and see how Michael's doing."

We didn't have a phone then. And it was nearly four in the morning so we couldn't go banging on a neighbour's door. So my dad walked down to the payphone, called in the report, and walked home.

He had just returned when the police arrived. It being Christmas night, things were slow, and they seemed eager for the action. They interviewed Michael without trying to get him too upset, and tried to transport him to a hospital, but he was having none of it. Then detectives poured over the scene of the crime. The highly experienced detectives had never seen anything like it in their careers.

"How much is there?" my Dad asked one of them.

"Only counting the neatly stacked notes of new currency in the boxes upstairs, we think it comes to around £24,000. Obviously, the old money will add to that, and the spilled notes, once we tidy them and count them."

So Michael had around three times the value of the house my family was living in stuffed under an old blanket. And he slept in piss while rats ate his bread and sugar at night.

Michael had been collecting his pension since he retired from the watchmaking game in the 1950s, and he'd been allotting himself the bare minimum for tea, sugar, bread and butter. The rest of the cash went into a box, under a bed, under a blanket. No one understood why. It didn't make sense to anyone that he'd live in such dire conditions while he saved a fortune.

Two days later, a detective called to our house to let us know they'd caught the robbers.

"Jaysus, that's great," said my Dad. "How'd you nab them? Fingerprints?"

"Not exactly," said the detective. "Some of these cases are easier than you'd think. We got a call from the Bank of Ireland on Talbot Street this morning. Two lads were asking to change old money. Fucking eejits. No one's changed old money in 15 years. We told them to stall them—tell them 'no problem, we just need to count it.' We got there in three minutes and took them in."

Sure enough, Michael's relatives arrived the following day, and we don't know exactly what happened after that, but anyone could rightfully guess. I think my dad always did, in some small way, regret not slipping a few pounds into his pocket that Christmas night.

But a few years later, when Michael passed away, he made his way into the house from the back garden and extracted the only item of value and beauty left in that house—a gorgeous cast iron fireplace with a high mantle from Michael's front room—the room he had lived in for decades.

When we moved a few years later, we took that mantle with us. It was given new life with a full restoration and installed into the hearth in our new living room. It was nice having Michael in permanent residence.

6

DUGGIE

Working for Uncle Paul could have been worse. Walking away from the printing on a Friday evening, after a week's work, with forty pounds to spend, was doing better than most of my mates. But that was primarily because most of my mates didn't have jobs, except the ones who were working for Paul, through my introduction. I should have gotten a finder's fee for bringing in Niall and Sean, but that wasn't how it worked with Paul. Those kinds of rewards weren't ever on offer.

We arrived at All Print and Design, Inc. a bit before 9 a.m. on the first Monday after our Inter Cert exams had finished: June 29th, 1987. This was to be put-your-head-down-and-get-shit-done-and-get-handed-cash-on-a-Friday work. Although I'd helped Paul out in the past, it was, as I'd come to realize, charity. But we were real teenagers now, and Paul had shit he needed done. There were jobs needing completion, and we were to be the final hands to touch the product before sending it out to the clients.

Maria sat inside the half-shuttered façade. She answered the phones, but her real job was keeping clients away from Paul by telling them that he wasn't there and she didn't know where he was.

She waved at me, smiled, and opened the glass door from the inside.

"Hiya!" she said to me, exuberantly. A little too much pep in her step for this early on a Monday for any of our likings. "And who are your friends?" I made the introductions.

"Paul's in back." She gestured with a nod of her head for us to go through to the warehouse as she ran to catch the ringing phone. "Pascal—howareya? No, he's not in yet. He said 11 but who knows?"

"Alright lads, Niall, isn't it? And Sean? Yeah, brilliant. Let's get you set up over here, lads." Paul shouted over the din and rattle of the AB Dick printing press and gestured to a couple of 6-foot long fold-out tables with a fold-out chair for each of us. There was a radio on way too loud, for the benefit of the row of aul wans, some of whom had been working since 6 a.m., some of whom would work 12 hours per day. With the amount of finishing work needing to be done, Paul was happy to provide as much work as they were willing to do. Overtime was always on offer, and with mouths to feed at home, almost all the employees availed of it daily.

The work at All Print and Design, Inc. consisted of slightly differing tasks, all mind-numbingly boring and replete with sure-fire repetitive stress injury. The women needed a distraction given the drudgery that print finishing entailed. There was a kettle for tea, and as long as whoever was making the tea made it quickly and distributed it around fast, Paul was willing to let that slide.

Heat raising (the bumpy ink on business cards) had to be done in a timely manner, right after the product came off the printing machine and the ink was still warm. We'd take the business cards (it was usually business cards), run them through the heat-raising dust, knock the rest of the dust off, and run them through the heat-raising machine, which was like a giant broiler with a belt running under it. The heat was terrible, and I'm sure the powder was carcinogenic. We'd stand there and toss coated cards into the machine forever.

For collating work, we organized the pages of Purchase Order books. Each page of the books were printed in three colors—white, blue, yellow. Our task was picking up a white page, printed with its order number "000001", then a blue and a yellow page with the same number, each from a pile of ten or twenty thousand. We'd take the three pages, place them face down on the desk and execute for number "000002". Any mistakes would be obvious (numbers out of sequence) and we'd have to lay the pages back out into their stacks until the number sequence was resolved. It happened to me many times, and the trick was to fix it before Paul found out.

Folding menus was our first assignment at Paul's. It was hard to fuck up. We'd take each page and fold it in half and place it in a pile. When we had enough, we'd put them in a box.

"Hurry up, the Chinese restaurant was promised them last week. We need them done today," said Paul. 30,000 menus. Folded in half. My mates, rife with newly acquired energy, were having a laugh. But as I'd been around the printing factory more than five minutes, I knew this was a week of work for us. We were going to sit there and fold these fucking menus for a week. Paul would placate the Chinese restaurant with a couple boxes of menus (all we had produced between the three of us that first day on our slow start). But he'd make Maria do it, and he'd make her charge them for a partially complete job, because he hated dealing with customers, and irate ones even more so.

This was the bulk of it. There was no intellectual challenge to it, and given Gay Byrne was consistently on the radio, there was no intellectual distraction either. It was rough going, but the first week came and went, and Paul, in his weird little way, called us into the office on the side of the printing factory floor, one by one, to pay us —in cash. One pound per hour. Forty pounds for the week. Most definitely less than any other wage we could have made anywhere else. We might even have been better off at the Chinese restaurant whose menus we folded all week. We checked with each other:

"Did you get forty?"

"Yeah, you?"

"Yeah."

"That was a bit weird then."

"Just the way he does it, I suppose," I said.

* * *

PAUL OWED all the success of the business to Father Frank Dunnigan. Duggie, as he was referred to by his peers and those within his tight orbit, continued to maintain a solid interest in All Print. He showed up maybe twice a week, flirted with the women working the print finishing (which they loved), attempted to flirt with Maria (who was having none of it), and eventually sequestered into Paul's office.

"Duggie! C'mere to me, howareya?" Paul would say as he brought him in close for a hug.

"Ah Jesus, Paul, alright. Alright."

I always found it fascinating that he took the Lord's name in vain. Not that I personally cared—I didn't believe in God. It was just interesting to me how Duggie comported himself; he always wore the collarino, and his suit was always just as dapper as could be. My mam had told me he'd gotten one of the parishioners pregnant in Seville Place, his home parish, and I didn't doubt it. He was a good-looking man in his mid-50s. I bet the aul wans were mad for a bit of him.

Duggie had taken Paul under his wing once he had left school. As the story goes, Duggie had an old flatbed letterpress in the presbytery. The parish had a constant need for pamphlets, flyers, and epistles, and Duggie roped Paul into assisting with jamming those out. Before long, Paul was a dab hand at the laborious task of arranging the letters (backwards) to create any word-based design. So it wasn't long before the local dry cleaners, auto shop, and bookies were hot for Duggie and Paul's printing services. They recognized the opportunity and went into business together.

Duggie financed an AB Dick printing machine—a serious step up from the old flatbed letterpress—and secured a small back office space. There was just one more element to All Print that was not apparent to most of the congregants Duggie regularly administered to: as well as Uncle Paul's business partner and co-owner of All Print and Design, Inc., he was also a bookkeeper.

Paul ran the day-to-day. The printing machines in the warehouse hummed along under his supervision. He routinely checked random samplings to ensure the operators were executing the jobs with precision. Chinese restaurant menus were run on the basic machines, whereas the more complicated jobs ran on the half-million-pound machines that had been financed through the bank and had to run almost continuously to pay for themselves and eke out a small profit for the business. When the smaller machines didn't have a job on, Paul would load them up with plates for coupons for All Print and Design, Inc.—leaflets to distribute around town, usually under car windshield wipers. The coupons would proclaim '15% off your first job at All Print and Design, Inc.' Typically, a group of us 15-year-old boys were instructed on exactly which areas of town to cover, and how to get from one to the next on the DART train. The best days were when Paul would send us out with train fare and a million All Print coupons to distribute. Anything to get out of the factory for a day.

Nothing ever appeared improper at the printing, as we called it. Except, at a stretch, Paul's inability to manage timelines and expectations for clients. But in all honesty, this dysfunction only appeared normal. What business didn't have issues with incompetent management, workplace trysts, and petty fighting amongst the employees? Whatever was going on below the surface was invisible to us. Customers came and went, jobs were printed and finished, and more importantly for all of us, Paul called every one of us into his office at the end of the day on Friday and paid us in cash. No one knew what anyone else was getting paid, except for us three lads because we were each getting the same pay regardless.

Paul was only ten years older than me but hated to see himself as an older uncle. There was a boys' club he used to take me to when I was eight and he was 17 or 18. Going in the first day, he warned me not to reveal I was his nephew. . When kids asked how we were related, I was to explain that we were cousins. "Do not fucking tell them I'm your uncle."

* * *

"Forty quid, right?" said Uncle Paul.

"Yeah, forty quid, boss," I said in his office at the end of the week.

He also hated when I called him boss, so the final minutes of a Friday was a safe time to pull that one out of the bag.

"What are you and Niall and Sean doing now? After this?"

"Eh, I don't know," I stuttered. This was new. What were we doing? What did he care?

Paul handed me my wagesand reached into his desk drawer and pulled out another large wad of notes.

"I need a favor," he said, as he started peeling ten-pound notes off and counting them silently with the barest movement of his lips, like a ventriloquist. He looked at me, waiting for an answer.

"A favor," he repeated.

It was as if the favor was to be granted. It was a foregone conclusion in his mind that whatever it was, we'd be taking on this errand on this particular Friday after work. Like a wave breaking over me, it became apparent that not only was this favor to be granted to him, but it would be paid handsomely—three ten-pound notes.

"Thirty quid. That's for you boys, alrigh'? That's more than an extra day's pay each, so I need you to take this seriously. Father Dunnigan is waiting for these leaflets in the presbytery. He needs them for confessions tonight." Paul nodded at a small duffel bag on the ground beside his desk.

"Ok," I said. "Bring these to Father Dunnigan in the presbytery. No problem, boss," I said.

"Shut the fuck up," he said.

* * *

On the way to the bus, I handed the lads their extra tenner, and savored the moment as their expressions went from confused, to delighted, and back to confused.

"What the fuck?" asked Sean.

"Yeah man, what's this for?" asked Niall.

"Simple," I said. "We're going to deliver these leaflets to Duggie. It's an end-of-week bonus for helping with this delivery."

"Your stingy fucking Uncle Paul is paying THREE of us to make a delivery. Does that not seem a bit odd?" asked Niall.

"I don't know. Who cares? We got a tenner each for it. Don't ask questions," I said.

"Fuck that, I have a question," said Sean. "Why didn't he just have his little lapdog Maria do it? She does everything else for him."

"Look, I don't know. Would you prefer to give him back the tenner? Should we go back to All Print and give him back the money and ask him why we're delivering these leaflets to Duggie and suggest that Maria do it for free?"

Niall grabbed the duffel. "Give me that fucking bag," he said as he swung it up on top of a rubbish bin. Grabbing the zipper, he started to peel it open.

"What are you doing?" I asked. "I don't think we should be fucking around with it."

"Yeah?" asked Niall. "Fitzer, if I'm going to deliver something to someone, I want to know what it is."

Niall whipped back the top flap of the bag. We all leaned forward in anticipation of what secrets the black duffel heading from The Boss to The Priest would hold.

Leaflets. Literally just the leaflets we had seen coming off the AB Dick press earlier that day—the same ones we had folded by hand.

"Church leaflets, Niall. Can we fucking go now?" But Niall wasn't satisfied. He rummaged beneath the leaflets, and a smug smile crept across his lips.

"Not down here," he said.

As he withdrew his hands, he grabbed an entire stack of church leaflets, and as he peeled those away, he revealed the contents at the bottom of the bag. The delivery we weren't supposed to see. Banknotes, carefully bundled with the little piece of paper around them and everything. Fifty-pound notes. Probably thousands of pounds in currency. We stood stunned for a moment, but this was not a Dublin neighborhood where you'd encourage strangers to learn that you were carrying a half a year's salary in a duffel bag.

"Put the fucking leaflets back in, Niall," I said.

He stood there baffled by the discovery. Sean grabbed the leaflets and the currency from him, smashed them back into the bag, and zipped it up quickly.

"Let's go," he said.

"Yeah," I said. "But keep it calm and cool. Normal pace. No need to look weird or anything. Everything's cool. Everything's normal."

"What the fuck?" whispered Niall. "What the fuck? What the fuck?"

"You're a fucking nob end. Wasn't it easier when we didn't know and we just got an easy tenner?" Sean was livid at Niall, but at the situation also. We walked to the presbytery, reminding each other to keep a relaxed pace. No one else knew, but it felt like the whole of Dublin was staring at us.

"Why would your uncle have us carry this cash?" asked Niall. "Like, why is he trusting in us? Something about this doesn't make sense."

"I know what you mean," I said. "Why not drive it down? Wouldn't that be much safer?"

"Maybe he can't get caught with it. Him or Duggie. Maybe there's something major happening. Maybe he and Duggie are being tracked by the Special Branch, and he needed this money down there tonight, but they know they're being watched so they can't transport it. Jesus fucking Christ, what are we involved in?" said Niall, thoroughly freaking out.

By now, the paranoia had started to bubble up and overflow our cups. What was the money for? Was it Provo money? Was it destined to head up North so the IRA could purchase weapons or bombs? Was the printing factory a front for a money laundering operation? Or maybe both of these things were true. Duggie was from Armagh, a stronghold of Provisional IRA activity, and some members of the church were well known to be sympathizers of the cause.

How much money was in the bag? It had to be tens of thousands. Maybe more. Were we carrying a quarter of a million pounds?

Unfortunately for us, our only choice was to deliver the bag to Duggie and somehow, miraculously, try to feign ignorance.

* * *

We were silent turning into Seville Place from Amiens Street. The parish church and Duggie's presbytery were just minutes away now, and we were unlikely to encounter anyone else, let alone anyone we'd be concerned interacting with.

"How are we going to hide from Duggie that we know what's in this bag?" I asked my two mates, who looked like they were experiencing a mixture of rage and terror.

"Who gives a fuck?" asked Niall. "In fact, I don't know what you need me for now. I might just bail and let you two take it from here."

"Bollox. You got a tenner for this. You insisted on opening the fucking bag. You're more responsible to deliver this than anyone. If I'm sticking it out, so are you," said Sean.

"So what are we gonna do about Duggie? He's gonna know," I said.

"Here's what we're gonna do," said Sean, "we're gonna smile nicely, hand him the bag, as nice as you like, and we're gonna say see ya later, and turn and leave."

"Great plan," I said. "Great fucking plan."

A minute later the three of us stood at the door to the presbytery. We decided that as Paul had asked me to deliver the bag, I would be the one to make the final handover. I prayed for it to go smoothly. Just let him take the bag, I asked God. Just let us get out of here quickly. I'll never do anything bad again. I rang the bell and waited and tried to breathe, but breathing started to feel like hyperventilating, so I tried consciously to slow it down. This ended up looking really weird, like a kid who was trying to hide something. Eventually Duggie answered the door.

"Ah lads! With the leaflets!"

He only needed a beat to recognize what we could never hide. We knew what was in the bag, and we were absolutely terrified. I held out the bag to him, but with what must have been sales dev training from a previous lifetime, Duggie ignored it. I desperately wanted him to take it from me. Why was he so nonchalant about this profoundly important bag?

"Are you lads ok?" asked Duggie.

"Yeah, here's the leaflets," I said, still holding the bag out for him to take, as if stating that it contained leaflets would somehow make it true.

Duggie stepped out onto the path in front of the presbytery and looked up and down the street.

"Were yis followed, boys? Did you notice anyone following yis?"

Fuck. We were fucked now.

"No," we all chimed in unison, with Niall adding, "Why would anyone follow us?" and Sean asking, "What would we be followed for?"

"I think yis know why," said Duggie. "Step inside. Quickly. QUICKLY." he uttered in that stern voice that priests learn in seminary, the tone that reminds their flock just who's in charge of their mortal souls.

* * *

Once inside the presbytery, Father Dunnigan handed the bag to a junior priest, asked him to take it to his chambers, unpack it, and make sure the contents were 'in order'.

"We didn't mess with any of it," Niall blurted out.

"No, I'm sure you didn't, son," said Duggie. "However, we're going to check carefully. Now, lads. Are you sure no one followed you down here from All Print? We can't take any chances. If anyone saw you, you'd have to stay here in the presbytery tonight so they don't follow you home."

There was a volley of "absolutely not" and "we're 100% sure" responses because there was no fucking way we were staying with Father Dunnigan for the night.

"Alright, alright. I'll have to take your word for it then," said Duggie. "As you obviously know what's in that duffel, I have to say this—you absolutely cannot tell anyone what's in that bag. It needs to remain a secret between Paul, the Church, and now you three lads. Do I need to explain the ramifications of this information becoming public? Are we clear?"

Another volley of "No" and "Yes" in response to the last two questions that ran somewhat concurrently, because all we wanted to do was get away from this terrifying situation. Ten minutes later, we were on our bus together heading home for the weekend, in total silence.

Niall, Sean, and I didn't speak that weekend, and I wasn't sure I'd see them at the printing on Monday. To be more precise, if they hadn't shown up, I wouldn't have been at all surprised. So I was happy when, at 9 a.m. Monday morning, at All Print and Design, Inc. on Parnell Street in the heart of Dublin's Northside, I found my two good friends waiting to punch their one-pound-per-hour clock again—and possibly with desires to run favors at a slightly better pay rate too.

As we set up our table and chairs and awaited instruction from Paul, Father Dunnigan arrived. He and Paul embraced, and had a private laugh between them. We figured that over the weekend Duggie had told Paul about us looking in the duffel. I thought we were done with running errands for Paul now, and thought that that was shite as any additional pay and any excuse to get out of the factory was key to our sanity.

"Give me a second, Duggie," we heard Paul say as he wandered over in our direction.

"Alright lads? Going to have you just do All Print leaflets under windscreen wipers today, ok? There's not much print finishing to do."

Absolutely brilliant, I thought. I'm sure we all thought.

"The leaflets are in my office, on my desk. Just grab them and stack them neatly in the duffel on the floor. Yous can carry it between yis. Just cover the usual territories, ok?"

"No problem, Paul."

I wanted to say 'boss' so bad, but it was early on Monday, Duggie was hanging out, and I didn't want to appear disrespectful, especially after the debacle from Friday. Better to keep my mouth shut and revel in this opportunity to get out of the printing factory all day and get paid for it.

Niall, Sean, and I headed into the office to pack up the leaflets, but instead we were surprised to see more fifty-pound notes stacked in neat bundles, covering most of Paul's desk.

But this time something about the cash looked off. Fifty-pound notes weren't in high circulation at that time, especially if you consider that a week's wages for us wasn't even fifty pounds. So we never saw them in circulation. But still, these looked off. They seemed bigger than a normal note, and the color was deeper, a little darker.

From the printing floor we heard Paul shout "Turn one over, *boss!*"

I poked my head out of the office, and over the clack of the presses I asked, "Wha?"

"Turn one over, *boss!*" he repeated, he and Duggie smiling ear to ear.

I returned to the desk, peeled a note from its stack, turned it over, and read:

ALL PRINT AND DESIGN, INC.

15% off your first order

'It's like printing money'

01 681 254

7

MT. WHITNEY

They say all mountain climbing comes with risk. Even on a not-so-terribly-tall mountain, or a climb that's more of a hike than anything technical, a lot can go wrong. A twisted ankle or head injury from a slip are common in the wilderness. Climbing or hiking with friends provides a partner or two to help assess the situation and hopefully splint the twisted ankle, or compress the head wound, and help the climber back down to civilization.

Possibly the most pernicious of all mountain ailments is AMS, acute mountain sickness. At first it feels like a throbbing headache but then quickly develops into a debilitating one. The only move is to stop, drink water, and take ibuprofen. If the headache goes away, you may climb on. If it doesn't, you may opt to continue climbing. But at this point, you've got to be completely honest with yourself. You're likely going to spoil someone else's climb in another 500 feet of altitude if you don't accept reality. You must descend, and it's wise to do so as quickly and safely as possible. Hopefully there is enough daylight left for you to see your way off the mountain. Before you start down, you should have an honest conversation with your climbing group to see if anyone else is suffering, because there's no point in leaving another injured climber—someone with a case of AMS so bad they're no longer able to walk—in the dark, on a mountain, in the nighttime cold air, ultimately needing another person to bring them down.

This might all sound very dramatic, but accidents happen on the world's most benign peaks every year. On Mt. Shasta, in 2023, there were four deaths and sixteen successful rescues. In 65 years, around 400,000 people have attempted to summit Mt. Rainier, resulting in 100 deaths. That's only 1/50th of 1%, but would you pause to consider that between one and two climbers die every year on this mountain before you slung on your crampons?

Mt. Whitney, the highest peak in the lower 48 states of the USA, also records one to two deaths per year. However, this did not figure into my decision when I agreed to climb Mt. Whitney with several friends in 2003.

It's the weirdest things I remember from that trip. My climbing partner, Mark, and I consumed a load of tasty bites for dinner, and he farted so badly all night that I literally couldn't sleep. I mean, it sounds funny but not sleeping the night before a 2 a.m. start on a summit attempt was absolutely brutal.

It was actually the afternoon before the ill-fated boil-in-the-pouch Indian food incident that I remember most—not just about this trip, but about any climbing trip I've ever been on. Mark and I, and four more Irish lads, had completed the first day's climb up Whitney. We arrived at the camping area known as Trail Camp at 12,000 feet, dropped our packs, and decided to have a little break before the work of pitching tents and boiling chickpeas commenced.

We were in great spirits. We had trekked a solid six miles up the trail and gained 4,000 feet of elevation. We had 3,000 still to climb over the course of around three miles, so life was about to get steeper and harder. But again, that was for later that night, starting at 2 a.m. With any luck, we would summit not long after dawn. For now, the objective was to gain back as much energy as possible by relaxing for an hour.

"What's that?" Mark asked, pointing up the mountain.

He was indicating the very top of an infamous stretch of the Whitney climb known as the switchbacks. There were either 99 or 100, depending on who you asked, and to be honest, when you're climbing them at that altitude, and you feel like you're dying, no one cares how many there are. You just want them to end.

"Oh yeah," I said. "That's a bit weird, isn't it? Like, is that one huge person, or several people bunched together?" It was really hard to see exactly what was happening at well over a mile away with the naked eye. Almost immediately, a helicopter flew over our campground, then over the blob on the mountain above us, and over the ridge beyond.

"Hey, excuse me!!" I hollered at a guy walking in the downhill direction. He was using poles, had a backpack on, and was moving fast. I figured him for a summiter on the way down, probably not wanting to get caught up here at sunset. I thought he might be privy to whatever was going on up the hill.

"Excuse me," I said. "Sorry, but do you know what's going on up there?"

"Yeah, some lady had a heart attack. Her group is trying to get her down here to Trail Camp. I think the chopper is trying to land to extract her."

"Oh fuck," I said. "Is she pretty bad?"

"She's conscious, actually. They've been carrying her down from the summit."

"Alright, man. Thanks for the info. Safe down."

"Yeah, you too."

* * *

So, wow—drama on the slopes. With absolutely nothing any of us could do, besides cast a magic spell to cure this woman of her ailment, we simply sat back and wondered if the chopper would find a place to set down. Indeed, it did, about a half mile up the mountain from where we were currently debating whether to end our glorious rest, pitch a tent, and make some food.

It seems mental to continue on as normal when a person is potentially dying, but again, this is one of the bizarre elements of climbing: there is nothing you can do. Either go home, or shut the fuck up and get on with your own climb.

"Excuse me?"

We all looked up. Just another climber, with the same $300 hiking boots and Arc'teryx gear we all had. What does this guy want? Maybe he's got questions about the mountain rescue.

"Yeah?"

"Yeah, I'm sorry to bother you guys. My girlfriend is unconscious in our tent. She's been that way for most of the day now, and I really need some help."

"I'm sorry, did you say unconscious?"

"Yeah."

"Sorry... for most of the day? What does that mean, 'most of the day'?"

"We left LA really early— like 3 a.m.—and got here around six. We only have a 24-hour permit, so we wanted to try to climb it in that window. We've been here since lunchtime, but she had been feeling weak for the whole climb. Actually, to be honest, after we pitched the tent she started throwing up blood."

He paused. It was obvious he wanted to say something else, but either wasn't sure if he should, or was embarrassed.

"Um. She's been shitting blood too."

"For fuck's sake. Are you serious? Where's your tent?"

"Just down here," said the man—Jeremy, I'd learn.

"Jeremy, why didn't you descend?" I asked. He muttered some

excuse. It didn't matter. It's like asking a shooting victim why they were in a particular neighborhood—it doesn't really matter now. There was only one thing to do: get to a hospital. If it was pulmonary or cerebral edema, the thing to do was get to a lower altitude. To not do so meant death.

* * *

We had all tried reviving the girlfriend, Anna, to absolutely no avail. And we'd steeled ourselves for the only resolution to this utterly shit scenario: Anna was going to need a bunch of people to carry her down the mountain; she'd have to be extracted, just like the lady in the chopper. It was going to absolutely fucking suck, as anyone who's tried carrying the dead weight of another human will attest.

I, like Anna, had had a pounding headache the entire climb up —a result of the altitude, I'm sure—but unlike Anna, I hadn't lost consciousness. But mountaineers adhere to a code: we help each other in times of trouble. Except in the highest of altitudes, like Everest, where a dying man cannot be moved by any other number of people. He must find the resolve to move himself, or perish.

So it was our duty to save Anna and abandon our summit bid. As we tried to figure out how we were going to pull this off, my mate Mark simply said, "Wait—the chopper." We looked at him and it dawned on us, one at a time, that there was a ride leaving the mountain just a half mile north of us. We just don't know when, and had no way of telling it to wait.

The chopper. The fucking chopper.

We had to get her to that chopper before it left. But it was a solid half mile away, and we had no idea how close the heart attack victim was to being loaded up and flown out. It was the only way to get Anna to a hospital, though. If we tried descending the trail, we'd certainly not make it to the trailhead—several hours away—before dark. And that was *if* we made it there at all. It would be a feat of incredible endurance for us four Irish lads plus Jeremy to get Anna down the mountain.

The chopper was the only way.

"We gotta make this happen immediately," I said. "We need a stretcher. What's her backpack like?"

"Yeah, it'll work," said Mark.

"Empty it," I said. "Everything. We don't need to carry any additional weight. All the pockets. Make sure it's completely empty." I watched him pull her personal items out, imagining her packing it just a day earlier, contemplating the summit that just about everyone managed to reach.

We were extremely concerned for Anna. She was totally unconscious, and we could do nothing to revive her. We unlaced her heavy hiking boots, useless now. There was not much else of weight to shed, so we dragged her out of the tent, managed to get her on her side, placed the backpack behind her, and rolled them both into a horizontal position. We each grabbed a strap like it was a handle.

The climb up that half-mile with each lad on a corner of the backpack was an hour of brute effort. My head was pounding; the altitude illness that Anna had ignored was back with a vengeance in my own skull. Until that point, this was the most immediate emergency I had ever dealt with, on or off a mountain.

One thing we knew for sure: if we didn't get Anna off the mountain, she would die—if she wasn't already dead.

* * *

Finally, we arrived at the chopper—and, incredibly, met the emergency crew coming down the slope.

"Who the fuck is *this*?" the medical tech demanded. She'd climbed with the rescue team and was just returning.

"Eh, Anna. This is her boyfriend, Jeremy. Anna's been unconscious since this morning. Earlier, she was throwing up blood."

"Jesus fucking Christ, get a pulse on her. Do you know how to get a pulse?"

I did, and I searched her wrist, but I couldn't find one. I was frankly scared of the medic. I didn't want to admit I was failing at such a simple task, but eventually I stammered, "I, uh, I can't find one. I don't think she has one."

"Of course she has one. Let me do it." She moved me aside with sheer authority, and spent a full minute checking herself.

As the small crowd stood around wondering what was going to happen next, Jeremy fainted.

"Get a pulse on *him*!!!" she bawled at Mark. He sprang into action.

"She doesn't appear to have a pulse—you're right. ... Oh wait. I've got something. It's weak, but she's alive."

'THANK FUCK,' we all thought silently.

By this point, the chopper pilot was leaning out the side of the bird, essentially screaming:

"I cannot fly at night! I'm not licensed! Daylight is almost gone —we need to leave *now*!"

Two minutes later, the heart attack victim and two additional patients were bundled in with the medic. The rotors came to life. We retreated. Thirty seconds later, the helicopter was too far from the mountain for us to even hear it anymore.

Would they be okay? I think we all wondered, standing there watching the helicopter move in that strange, crab-walk flight pattern they all seem to—lifting off and flying sideways before finally pointing toward home.

Three people. One who had had a heart attack—but stable. One who'd just passed out. And Anna—barely alive.

It was a weird night at camp. We were solemn, but light-hearted because we needed to keep our spirits up. At 2 a.m., we'd wake and attempt an additional 3,000 feet to the summit—then 3,000 back to base camp to break down, and 4,000 back to the trailhead. A monumental day of climbing.

I was sorry Anna ended up the way she did. These climbs require preparation and education.

I wonder what the AMS felt like for Anna, as it first manifested. Probably just like mine, a low-grade headache. I knew the signs, I drank extra water and took some ibuprofen. I wonder what she was doing as the headache began to pound in the back of her head. Did they get to pitch their tent before she threw up? Did she try to hide her symptoms from Jeremy, so as not to disappoint?

The summit was hard. I couldn't really get them out of my mind. My head was throbbing, and every step felt like a sledgehammer to the dome. I didn't want to end up like our friends from L.A., so I swore if it got worse, I'd turn back. But this wasn't Everest. It was a 15,000-foot peak—only a few hours of strenuous hiking. So the plan was: no matter how bad it got, keep going. As soon as I started down, it would get better.

Congratulations were had at the top. We descended quickly—there was no need to hang about. It was time to pack and get off the mountain before dark, 16 hours after our 2 a.m. start.

With tents and bags on backs, we made one last check of camp and turned for home.

I felt like the trauma of the previous day was behind us—until we found ourselves in front of Jeremy and Anna's abandoned tent.

"I hope they made it," said Mark. No one responded. We all knew that was a "Yeah" from each of us.

I spent weeks after the trip trying to figure out what happened to them. I scoured newspaper articles from L.A.—hoping not to find one. Nothing ever came up.

Climbing mountains is first and foremost a challenge of fitness and tenacity, in equal parts. One must be fit for the task and have the mental fortitude to be unwilling to quit, no matter how tough the going gets. But there's other aspects to it - the ability to calmly assess one's current situation in relation to fitness and desire, sure. But also other variables, like incoming inclement weather, dropping temperatures as the sun sets and night begins to fall, food reserves, and equipment. What is happening now, what's to come in an hour? Overnight? Tomorrow? Lastly, and most importantly, how must I weigh the risk of continuing versus the much lower risk of quitting and going home? Summit fever is real, and it's a killer. The mountain will always be there tomorrow.

8

THE WARD

"Mr. Sheridan. Mr. Sheridan, are you with us?"

"What's his CIWA score, nurse? Meds?"

I opened my eyes to the usual crowd of mental health professionals standing around my bed. I'd seen this scene play out before. Several interns, the charge nurse, and of course, the doctor in charge, surrounded me.

"He's a 16 Dr. Manfred. He had 2mg Lorazepam PRN last night on admission."

"Can you sit up for me so I can listen to your heart?" I could tell he was in a hurry. I wasn't the highest priority around here; I knew that to be the case. But I had my own agenda.

"Yeah, sure. I need to talk to you, Dr. Manfred. Listen, I know I drink too much, but I'm functional. I only drink and smoke weed to stop the madness in my head. That's what I need help with. I've been through every antidepressant on the market, and they all help for a couple of weeks, but then I just lose it again. I checked myself in here last night. I didn't come from a hospital."

"What do you mean you checked yourself in? That's not possible. You need an ER referral."

"My doctor, Dr. Hill, requested it. I told him I wasn't sure I'd

make it safely through the night, so he called the ward. He told me
to walk into the lobby and someone would be down to get me."

"Is this true?" the Doctor asked the nurse. "Dr. Hill called
him in?"

"I wasn't on last night, but that's what they said, yes."

"Never heard of that before." he muttered. "OK, I'll call Dr. Hill
later today and see what it is we're supposed to do with you." And
with that, the entourage moved on to the next room on the ward.

Psych wards run on routine. As much as the movies would have
you imagine, we weren't all running around waving our arms in the
air and making crazy sounds. This wasn't *One Flew Over the Cuckoo's
Nest*. Even though we were all stuck there until they let us leave, the
only similarities with that classic movie were that most of the
patients didn't want to leave. Mostly, they were patched up and let
loose onto the streets of San Francisco again, generally to return a
few days or weeks later. There were a few patients, like me, who
weren't your traditional homeless person with raving psychosis. We
really just wanted to get diagnosed, get into treatment, and get out
of there.

There was always a clear distinction amongst the patients:
those like myself, who were sick, and the lifers. We had something
wrong with us - depression, substance abuse, mental breakdowns.
We'd been dropped into this nightmare but were getting better and
we were getting the fuck out, ASAP. And actually, it wasn't a bad
place to be for a few days, or weeks, while they got your meds
sorted, and found you a therapist on the outside. Except for the
boredom. Fuck me, it was boring. But as this was my third stint in
as many months, I had come prepared. I had seven or eight books,
headphones so that I could listen to my phone whenever I
managed to smuggle it into my room (often), and a quite enormous
supply of weed edibles. These weren't your common and garden
5mg chewies, these were the 50mg, take-your-head-off, version.
And I shared them liberally with my new and temporary friends.

The lifers were obvious. Resigned. Some of them had been

dealing with traumatic illnesses, like psychosis, their entire lives, and many of them were here because they'd been abandoned by family, by society. They were caught in the revolving door of the psychological programs of whatever city or county they happened to be in. In this instance, they were in the city and county of San Francisco, and specifically, what's been said to be the best hospital for the mentally afflicted, Langley Porter at the UCSF Campus.

But would it work for me this time? I couldn't live the way I was living. And I was terrified that if this didn't work, I might never leave at all.

* * *

I emigrated to America on March 1st, 1992, but in many ways my journey began a couple of years before that. I mostly couldn't have helped the choices that led me to my ultimate escape from the Emerald Isle, and my lock down many decades later in Langley Porter.

At seventeen, I failed my high school final exams horrifically. At the time, I assumed it was due to some undiagnosed learning disorder, or test anxiety, or perhaps the first emergence of the illness I would wait nearly thirty years to have diagnosed, in the ward on the hill in San Francisco.

I went back to school the following year and retook the subjects I'd failed. This time I cobbled enough results together to achieve a passing grade. It meant nothing. There were barely any college-level courses I could apply for, let alone be admitted to with exam results like mine. College was for kids who got proper results, not dimwits like me. And yet somehow, a lower-level community college offered me a place in a communications course. I was definitely going to take the spot, too, but one of my best friends, Edwina, called from San Francisco and told me she was having the time of her life. Some other friends from her college years were already over there. There was work, parties, and friends. I needed to get out there as soon as I could, and everything would be taken care of. College, or adventure. I probably didn't know it at the time, but I was an adventure type of guy. I'd go on to travel and climb tall peaks, raft raging rivers, and land aeroplanes on glaciers. It didn't take too much pondering to decide to fly out to San Francisco.

This was around the same time everything changed for me. I was 18 or 19 years old, and a fog had descended. The excitement and joy of gathering with friends for music, or a night of deep conversation in a pub, or a bus trip down to some epic party in a small Irish town were disappearing. The anxiety at the thought of leaving the house and waiting for the bus into Dublin City Center, or the horrific anticipation of having to wait in a pub someplace if I happened to be first in the door, were starting to overwhelm me. I wish I'd known, and I wish I'd said something, but I didn't. So the invitations to come out to San Francisco, where several of my friends had ended up after graduating from various Irish colleges, seemed to be the perfect opportunity to escape Ireland, start a new life, and get away from the demons screaming at me from inside my head.

I'd run from them, that was for sure. I'd moved my physical body from Ireland to California. It was what the AA heads called a geographical cure. If you run fast enough and far enough, you might just escape the ghosts that surround your being, that infect your every thought with self-doubt and judgment. You can't, of course. That's not how it works. But landing in a scene rife with drugs and drink and all-night partying makes one realize that there are other ways of dealing with mental illness. It's simply a matter of self-prescribing, once the favorite elixir is discovered. And for me, that magical medicine was marijuana. A more potent version of the dope of the 60s, this modern day herb was tens of times stronger than the shit the hippies smoked on Haight Ashbury in the 1960s, literally two blocks from where I was staying in Edwina's madhouse.

I remember her greeting me off the super shuttle minibus at the curb as I arrived from the airport. She was so happy to see me, and happy in general. Edwina was, and still is, the absolute life of the party. Edwina knew everyone, and was the center of our social circle.

The first person I met in Edwina's was her upstairs neighbor, Jim. He loved to spend time in Edwina's because of all the adorable Irish boys that floated through. Jim had a special talent for massage. Actually, his special talent was more convincing the lithe Irish lads to come upstairs to his apartment for a free one. I got one myself, and that's how I know. It was alright, but really the point was a handjob, and if you weren't into that then it was just going to be a short back rub. Jim and his roommate, Steven, didn't talk. They lived at opposite ends of their tiny apartment, and I always wished I knew what the conflict was there. One day, Edwina told me Jim was in the hospital but didn't say what for. I don't think I asked. I just assumed it was something like a check up or a routine procedure. He just always seemed healthy. His stout stature, his full beard and ruddy cheeks.

But Jim never came home. He died of AIDS soon after, and I finally realized that he and Steven had been lovers. In all likelihood, one had passed the virus to the other, and while the relationship couldn't stand that strain, they were financially unable to move out of their apartment. Estranged lovers, hiding from each other in 800 square feet, waiting to die.

Jim's funeral was attended by a good crowd of people, at a venue in the Mission District that was there to support the gay and lesbian community in end-of-life circumstances. I remember a bird came careening through the service, during a speech. I think it was a black bird. It made so much noise. I caught Steven's eye and we both smiled. It was a beautiful acknowledgment of his former lover. Steven passed soon after, and his scooter sat on the street collecting street cleaning tickets every Tuesday and Thursday until one day it was towed, and the last worldly image of him disappeared forever.

* * *

These were the memories that pervaded my mind as I lay on my dorm-room-style bed, staring at the ceiling, waiting for 23 hours and 48 minutes to pass so I could get an updated report from the doctor. They'd run several tests on me, conducted psychological interviews, and explained longitudinal mood tracking. Would I undergo electric shock treatment? Yeah, sure I would. Anything at this point. Anything to find relief.

Three months earlier I'd been in the same state. Crying and shaking and wanting to die, I'd taken myself to a clinic. They 5150'd me, which I had no idea what that was, and admitted me for my first in-patient stint. Some experimentation with antidepressants and some mild success later, I was free again. I struggled through several more months; the drugs had stopped working, and I was boozing and everything else anyway, so not the path to success I imagined.

The next stint involved another facility stay. I wanted off that ward so badly I feigned health, and a week later, I was out. But I was not healthy, and that's what led me to the third, and final trip inside - this last one initiated by yours truly. I'd called my doctor late at night on December 31st, wondering if I'd see a new year, or if I'd be gone before the clock rang out the old one.

You see, I missed Jim. I missed Steven too, but Jim had really been my friend. It had been 25 years since he'd died in the early 90s, and I still missed his beautiful ways. He was everything this world needed: a gentle soul, and a quiet voice that everyone would shut up and listen to when he spoke, because he was smart, and so insanely funny. An older, sober gay man, he should have lived outside our scene of awfully young troublesome rabble rousers, but he fit right in. I wanted to fit into this world, too, but I couldn't any more. After decades of misuse, the drugs had stopped working and now they just made me sick. Just like the antiretroviral drugs Jim was taking, they just stopped working one day.

* * *

"Mr. Sheridan Mr Sheridan, are you awake?"

I wasn't awake. I'd dosed off reading Oscar Wilde. Thank God for the books I'd brought in, they were keeping me sane. I'd been daydreaming about whether Wilde had had me in mind when he wrote, in *The Picture of Dorian Gray*:

> "It's an odd thing, but anyone who disappears is said to be seen in San Francisco. It must be a delightful city and possess all the attractions of the next world."

I'd disappeared decades ago. I hid it well, but I'd faked my way through my life, relationships, even raising my disabled child, in order to treat the insanity that wouldn't leave me alone. I suppose it is a delightful city, and yes, offers the attractions of the next world. My weariness couldn't wait.

"Yes, doctor?"

Weird time of the day to be getting called on from the doctor. It was maybe somewhere between lunch and dinner.

"Mr. Sheridan, Dr. Hill is in my office. We'd like to speak to you now. Follow me, please."

The fuck? Ok, let's assume this is good news, and not 'we're kicking you out of here because your insurance won't pay any more.'

Dr. Manfred led me through the ward, and slipped his key into the lock that kept his brood safe and secure, and we ventured out into the hallway. It was the first time in 17 days I'd been outside, and the feeling of freedom was overwhelming. It was five steps to Dr. Manfred's office, and I savored every one of them.

"Good afternoon, Mr. Sheridan!" said Dr. Hill as I stepped inside the room. He gestured to a chair across from his desk.

"How have you been doing these last two weeks?" he asked.

"Well, you know, ok, but not great. I just don't feel like these new antidepressants are—"

"We know," he said.

I glanced at Dr. Manfred. He was looking at me with a slight twinkle in his eyes. Back to Dr. Hill.

"I need you to do something for me," he said. "Actually, you have to do this for me, because without your help I can't treat you any more."

"Ok," I said. Where was this going?

"We think we know what's wrong with you, Mr. Sheridan," Dr. Manfred said. He looked back at Dr. Hill like maybe he shouldn't be the one delivering this news.

"Dr. Hill?" I said.

"You have to get sober. I can't treat you unless you're sober. We're pretty sure you have Bipolar Type II Disorder. It requires 100% sobriety for successful treatment. The antidepressants were never going to work for you, because you're not depressed. We can talk about this at length at your first appointment in my office next week. We're going to get you on a medication protocol and within three days, we'll have some levels. By then you'll be feeling quite a bit better, and you'll be released. Get to AA, or NA, or both, I don't really care. But if you can't maintain sobriety, the medication won't work."

I spent the next three days in the ward wondering where the last 30 odd years had gone, but determined, for the sake of Jim, and Steven, and many more, not to let my incurable, but treatable, illness take another minute of my precious time away. As Wilde famously quipped, I could try to live: the rarest thing in the world.

9

MT. SHASTA

This happened a long time ago so some of the details are hazy. Some details, though, I will never forget. Let's start with the hazy ones: a bunch of mates were organizing a drive up north in an attempt to climb Mt. Shasta, and someone unfortunately called me to see if I'd like to go.

"Yeah, sure," I said.

I mean, what did I know? Was this a big hike, or was there truly some mountaineering to be had? I had no idea. But I said yes because that's what you do. You stick with your mates, all of whom were much fitter than I.

Other hazy details, like where the camping gear came from, or how I ended up with a pair of crampons and an ice axe, are forever lost to the winds of time. But end up with those things I did, and as we camped for the night next to the parking lot, I asked what the ice axe might be used for.

"Basically it's for arresting a fall," said Mark. "If you fall, you drive this pick into the snow or ice by placing your off-hand on the T of the axe."

"Then you push down hard and pray to fuck," said Rich, raising a round of laughs from our already excited and adrenaline-fueled compatriots.

Mark leaned over to me and, in a low voice, said, "Don't worry. When we reach camp tomorrow, I'll take you over to the slope and show you and let you get a bit of practice in."

"That'd be great," I said, still not fully understanding if this was an important skill to master before the climb or just something nice to know.

In the morning, we set off. We were a string of young, lanky Irish guys in our late 20s. Nothing could dampen our enthusiasm, and after several hours, we arrived at second camp in the late afternoon—the spot we'd launch our summit attempt from later that night. Tents needed pitching, food needed preparing, and if I'm being honest, this was the best possible time to take a crap, as having to navigate that on the very steep slopes the following day was to be avoided at all costs.

Considering the effort needed for our preparations, Mark's offer to practice some ice axe technique was basically set aside. And to be honest, as the weakest member of this fantastically fit group of young men, I was too tired to bother with it myself.

We left camp at an ungodly hour, maybe two or three a.m. Actually, it might even have been four a.m.—and by all accounts, that's way, way too late to leave for the summit. All I remember about that part is that we left too late, and after an hour of slow climbing, the stronger lads just left us behind.

The "us" was me and my mate Mark. Mark was fit and strong, but he'd been dealing with some kind of stomach bug, so that put him climbing at my pace.

It was a weird morning. One of the memories I'll never forget was feeling the presence of a climber to my right. I had a headlamp on, and when I looked over, I saw a shirtless man in tennis shoes, with no gloves. He was climbing on all fours, digging his hands into the snow, scooping huge mounds as he moved past us up the mountain. I must have looked in some state of shock, because he looked over and declared:

"CLIMBING FOR JESUS!"

It's one of those things that happens at altitude that you can't be sure actually happened—but I'm pretty sure it did.

Mark and I struggled all day. With me being completely out of shape, and his stomach woes, we were a great pairing on the slope. Beaten and broken, we eventually reached the summit and found our mates—well-rested after an hour and a half waiting for us.

"Jaysus lads, we weren't going to wait too much longer, but we have to get some photos of all of us together at the summit."

Snaps were had, and then the lads were gone. The sound of fresh snow under their crampons as they split was terrifying. Mark and I were feeling broken and somewhat abandoned, but we understood that it was kind of on us to get up and down this mountain ourselves.

We took a short break because having left late, and now having taken an age to reach the summit, we didn't want to get caught in darkness. And as the day wore on, we had to face increased danger from the loosened scree being shed by the mountain itself. So off we went, tired but motivated by the thought of a beer and a nice meal later that night.

I'm not sure where exactly on the descent it happened. I just remember that, for one brief moment, my right crampon—which had begun to feel like second nature—missed the mark in the ice. Instinct kicked in and I tried to regain my foothold, but with the utter exhaustion, it just didn't happen.

In a split second, I was parallel to the slope, sliding and picking up speed. I heard a skier someplace nearby, but realized almost immediately that the sound was actually my jacket and pants, hissing over the slick iced surface of the mountain. This would have been an appropriate time to scream, but instinct demanded that I reserve every ounce of concentration to attend to this situation.

I'm not sure I've ever truly understood the meaning of the word *instinct*, but I took my axe—having never even once practiced the technique—and placed my left hand on the T, gripped the handle with my right, and drove it into the ice. Nothing.

I was still sliding. I'll never know if that slide would have killed me, but I know for sure that, at that moment, I definitely thought I was about to die. I hadn't budgeted for dying on a fucking mountain. This was supposed to be recreation.

I continued to drive that axe into the ice—must have tried around ten more times. I was really moving now. I didn't think there was any way I would stop. My main concern quickly became the boulders that defined the terrain. There was no doubt in my mind that I was traveling fast enough now that striking a boulder square on would have tragic consequences—knocking me out to the extent that I would no longer even be able to self arrest. Instinct again had me rise up onto my knees. I tried to push my entire body weight through my knees into the ice and, at the same time, lessen my surface area. One more drive downward with the axe and I felt myself slowly coming to a stop.

I sat there for around 15 minutes. The sheer exhaustion made it literally impossible to stand up. And even if I could have, I didn't have the ability to climb back up to Mark.

I was shaking. Badly.

Eventually, though, we all have to go home. I spent an agonizing amount of time carefully securing my footholds on the ascent back up to the man with the dodgy tummy. When I reached him, he was ashen-faced.

"I didn't think you were going to stop," he said.

It's a sentence I will never forget. The tone of it. The delivery. The brutal honesty of a man who might have been even more shaken than I was at that moment.

"Let's get to the glissade," I said.

Not long later, we reached the glissade—an ice chute cut into the slope upon which you could slide a couple thousand feet down off the mountain to the camp spot. I turned my ice axe around and used it as a brake—and in less than 30 minutes, we were back at our tent. I'd just summited one of the tallest mountains in the U.S. and just barely lived to tell about it.

You'd think that would have warned me off climbing. But for some weird reason, the opposite happened. I don't think it was as simple as trying to recapture the adrenaline high from almost sliding off that slope—I ride motorbikes and whitewater raft regularly. I know how and where to get my rushes without approaching my demise. I honestly think my desire to climb did come from that first proper mountaineering experience, but it wasn't really tied to the accident. Like most climbers, I do it to get out into nature, for the physical challenge, and of course, the view. As John Muir famously stated "The mountains are calling, and I must go." Since then, I've climbed the tallest mountain in the lower 48—Mt. Whitney, in California—*twice*. Once I had a 24-hour permit where no camping was allowed. It was up and back in a day. It took 18 hours: over 20 miles one way with 7,500 feet of altitude gain, and the same in reverse to descend.

I've also stood on the summit of Mt. Kilimanjaro and felt that roof-of-Africa awe. For two weeks on the Annapurna Circuit in Nepal, I lived life on the trail. Next year, if I can get rid of this belly, I will attempt another of the Seven Summits—Mt. Aconcagua, in Argentina. At 22,837' it's the highest mountain on Earth outside of the Himalayan Range. This will probably be the crowning achievement in my mountaineering career.

So although I've definitely found something about facing my own mortality that's attractive, that's not the primary objective. Because whether it's a mountain or a story, the question is the same: *How far can I go—and still get home?*

10

THE BOY

I felt like I was wandering through a dream—everything moved in slow motion. Our future seemed to depend on this visit to the child psychologist. We sat in the waiting room in silence. Not just us, his parents, but the boy, too. Not a word. I wished he'd speak, but he didn't usually. And now, neither did his parents. This was the courtroom, and our family was about to receive a verdict that would either relieve us of our crushing concern, or condemn us to fearful decades or more of therapies, special schools, support groups.

"Hey buddy!" I said. "Luca! Whatcha doing?"

I slid off the couch that had seen decades of frantic parents, dry-mouthed and frozen, waiting for the call into the doctor.

I worked my way over to him.

"Whatcha doing?" I asked again. I wanted to prime the pump for the scrutiny I knew was coming soon. Spark an interaction. "That's a cool train! Who's driving that train, buddy? Where's it going?" *Speak. Please, please speak. If you don't they're going to cast you into a net, and us with you, and life won't be the same for us, buddy.*

"The doctor is ready for you now. Please come in."

The intern in the white lab coat beckoned us inside with a

broad smile. "He can bring the train in with him," she said, as she noticed me stalling and wondering what to do with the toy. "Come on, Lu," I said, "Let's go see the doctor. Maybe she's got other toys to play with?"

The doctor's office was in fact full of toys - from jigsaws and puzzles to scratch pads and crayons, and, of course, trains. Luca wasted no time in picking out a locomotive, and walked to the window where the shade was retracted just enough to be out of his reach. Mom was talking to Dr. Klumensan, answering some basic questions and discussing insurance. I was in a deep fog thinking, *This is going to be ok. He's ok. I mean, I know he's a bit in his own world, but look at him - he's fine.* I had a concern about Luca's age. Was he not a bit young for us to be meeting with the doctor for a concern like this? I turned my gaze from Luca who was staring out the window onto a downtown San Francisco street, the city of his birth just 18 months earlier, to the doctor.

"Dr. Klumensan, is he not a bit young . . . ?" but, her eyes on Luca, she cut me off by simply holding her hand aloft, palm out.

"Luca," she said, in a normal voice. No need for raised voices here, he'd already had his hearing checked, the first test we'd done to eliminate sensory deficit.

"Luca," again. I looked at him, staring out the window. *Come on, buddy. Fucking come on, turn around. Show the doctor that you're just in a developmental phase. You're normal, and you just need some help growing out of this.*

"Luca."

She made some notes but didn't give anything away. "Sorry, dad. I didn't mean to cut you off, it's just that it was a perfect moment for that test. What did you want to ask me?"

"Nothing," I said. "It doesn't matter."

My dream state continued, and it was at that exact moment I understood that his mother's suspicions for the past few months were correct. Our son was autistic.

* * *

Luca's mom knew early on because she recognized the signs. Luca's first word didn't come until he was nearly 15 months old. Agua. It took us a couple weeks to even figure out that's what he was saying. Every time we'd run the faucet in the kitchen sink he'd giddily start repeating "OW-WA! OW-WA OW-WA!!". Eventually I realized that his Spanish-speaking nanny had taught him to say 'agua'.

My wife had grown up with an autistic brother. Aspergers was what they called it back then - a phrase since retired clinically but used still colloquially. Roberto had been a great kid, by all reports. Mom's childhood with Roberto, absorbed into her every fiber, was the education she needed for recognizing Luca's traits early on. He loved locomotives, sure, and loved building the wooden train tracks for them using every available piece of track. But he also became frustrated if the tracks wouldn't stay together, or fell over, and then he would refuse to play with the trains and tracks together. That's not how those items were supposed to interact, according to him, no matter our encouragement to try it out. So tracks stayed built, and empty, and trains stayed connected with their magnets on the carpet beside them.

Roberto was writing a book on the history of the Second World War. It was three decades in the making so far, and clocking in at over a thousand pages. I wondered if Luca would produce a work of such deep knowledge and intense focus on a specific topic one day.

"Have you read Roberto's book?" I asked Giulia one day.

"I have not," she said.

"Why not?" I asked. "Are you not curious if it's any good?"

"Good? It's a thousand pages about World War II," she said. "I mean, I love my brother, but no one's got time for that."

"What if Luca writes a book like that someday?"

"Let's wait and see," she said.

The actual diagnosis took weeks to arrive, but by that point, he had started therapeutic treatment. From Speech Therapy to Advanced Behavioural Analytics, it was full on, with therapists in and out of our house on the daily, plus weekends fairly booked too. We even booked flights to Ireland so Luca could engage with his seven cousins, hoping that this would be some strong emotional bonding for him. In reality, we were filling a schedule. We were doing what we were told to do. "Early intervention is key, and you got an early diagnosis. You're lucky, get on it." they said.

* * *

Six months flew by, and Luca had his second birthday. We had it in the local park, and there was a mix of new moms and their infants (all of our friends seemed to be having babies all of a sudden) and kids from our newfound tribe of spectrum parents. The park was a great option as food and drink could spill and it didn't matter. I never in my life thought I'd dress my two year old in clothes to match mine, but we donned identical Irish soccer tops that my sister had sent over so we could represent Ireland in the World Cup.

"Jesus, Rossa, he's getting so big already," said my friend Lola.

"I know, it's insane. I can't believe he was so little when he was born. You know, I can barely hold him on my hip anymore."

"He's absolutely fearless on the slide and the spiderweb. I've never seen anything like it."

"Yeah, I wonder if it's a spectrum thing? I don't know. I was talking to another parent recently who said their kid was the same at this age. Fearless. It's actually something I need to watch. He fell off a play structure a few weeks back and landed on his arse. I had that moment—you know when you're expecting that three second pause before they realize they're hurt—but he never cried. It was a six foot drop but he just got up and kept running around."

"Boss man - forgive the interruption." Lola's husband Mohan interrupted gently. "We have to get our two to another playdate, but they're going mental for birthday cake. No pressure, but when are you planning on getting that going?"

"Oh. Yeah. Of course. I don't see why we can't do it now. LUCA!!! DO YOU WANT TO BLOW OUT CANDLES AND EAT CAKE NOW?"

Like most kids, sugar motivation was strong in my one, and he scrambled down and ran to us quickly.

* * *

We were tired, mom and I. Saturdays were always tough—a rush to get out of the house to an early appointment for a Floor-time session Luca absolutely loved. He adored the instructor, the other kids in his class, even the support staff. But it meant one of us trying to get Luca ready and dressed, and the other either making breakfast, or worse, driving to the local store for bagels and coffees. We'd grabbed the slot as soon as it became available, even though it was the first session of the day, and all the way across town in an area where parking was beyond tough. This was a coveted program, and we knew we'd be crazy not to take this spot, with the promise of moving into a more reasonably-timed session as it became available.

God, though, we were tired. I was holding it together and trying not to snap at her. I resented having to visit with her family and stay there overnight, when all I wanted was to steal away into the guest bedroom for six solid hours of sleep. And I wasn't any better with my increased drinking.

"Did you find the, em, thing?" I asked.

"The what?"

"The thing, Christ, I can't think of what it's called. I asked you to look for it a bit ago."

"Well if you can give me a better clue, I might be able to help. What's it for?" she asked.

"For strapping his car seat in on the plane."

"The lap belt extender. Yes. YOU found it and packed it into the carry on bag. Are you losing your memory or what?" she snapped.

I wasn't sure what was happening to me. Was I losing it? I was sure mom thought I was just under strain. Certainly, the prospects of flying with a young child ten and a half hours across the US and the Atlantic were frightening. We didn't have the kind of kid who liked to sit still, I mean AT ALL. I couldn't imagine how this was going to go once a couple minutes of reading distraction had worn thin.

* * *

This was his second trip to Ireland, the first having been when he was just a tiny baby. During Luca's childhood we would average one trip per year. He got to know his cousins closely, and as they were from ultra progressive households, their mams had trained them in how to communicate with Luca, and how to treat him as one of the family. They always included him in their games, when younger, and in running around the neighborhood as they, and he, got older. I remember my mam's delight at his American accent, which in turn delighted me, and my dad's made-up game of 'get out of jail' in the back garden where he'd corral all the kids into a 'jail' and pretend not to be paying attention so they could all 'escape' and run wild. Luca didn't really get that one, and needed my dad to motion him to run away with the other kids. Possibly a bit too conformist for that game.

"Look at him out there, running around with his cousins," my mam said to me, sitting at the kitchen table one afternoon, as my dad chased them around pretending to be a monster.

"Yeah, he absolutely loves it here, mam. He's never as happy as when he's here with his cousins."

"Would you not think of moving back with him, love?"

"To where? Here? Can we take the top bedroom? Mam, come on, it just wouldn't be possible. His mom doesn't want to live in Ireland, she's a lawyer - she can't work here. And his cousins love him, yeah, but this is all fun because there's an expiration date attached. We're leaving Sunday and everyone knows that. We'll be back again in a year, mam."

"I suppose. It's just great having you all home. We miss you over there."

They missed us over there. Not that they missed us and our non-neurotypical child. Just us.

* * *

One of the best and worst things anyone ever said to me regarding Luca's autism was from one of his therapists, a doctor who ran a program Luca attended:

"You know, Rossa, I wouldn't be surprised if Luca grew out of much of his behaviors as he ages. He's very mild on the spectrum. I'm fairly confident he will become more neurotypical in time."

"Wow. Really?" I asked.

"Yes. I think you'll see a difference by age 12 or so."

But the real change was mine. I stopped feeling the need to explain my child to strangers, and offer his diagnosis. I realized I didn't need to make excuses for him. Although, I never could quite get rid of the desire to stand close and watch for bullying, and to make sure Luca always got his turn in the playground.

We've certainly had our challenges these last dozen plus years. We moved from San Francisco to a tiny country town north of the city so that Luca could attend a school more suited to his needs. I worked through several severe health issues, always battling to get back home for my son and to support him as he grew. His mom always spearheaded the medical, insurance, and therapeutic component of Luca's care brilliantly. We're fighters. Life can be tough, but we battle to make it make sense, and we revel in the beauty therein.

Luca is an amazing teenager. I can't believe what a beautiful grown up he's becoming. To me he is normal, however that's defined. I love him so deeply. Life with him is full, rich, and beautiful.

ABOUT THE AUTHOR

Rossa Sheridan grew up in Ballybough, in Dublin's North Inner City. After emigrating to the USA, he lived a life of adventure, including climbing, traveling, adventuring, and having an amazing child. It was always his childhood experiences at home with his brother, and friends from the flats, that inspired his writing.

www.ingramcontent.com/pod-product-compliance
Lightning Source LLC
Chambersburg PA
CBHW051736040426
42447CB00008B/1155